The Book of Romans

The Expositor's Bible Study and Commentary

DR. MAXWELL SHIMBA

Shimba Publishing LLC
Printed in the United States of America

First Printing Edition 2023

Table of Contents

Preface

The Book of Romans

The Book of Romans, a profound and transformative letter within the New Testament of the Bible, stands as a cornerstone of Christian theology and a testament to the power of faith, grace, and redemption. Authored by the Apostle Paul, a fervent preacher and theologian of his time, Romans weaves a tapestry of profound insights, theological depth, and practical wisdom that has resonated through the ages.

This preface serves as an invitation to delve into the timeless and life-changing message of Romans. It encapsulates the essential themes, messages, and purposes of this magnificent epistle.

Historical Context and Authorship

Written in the mid-first century A.D., the Book of Romans emerges against the backdrop of a world where Christianity was a fledgling, persecuted faith. Paul, a Pharisee turned passionate follower of Christ, was uniquely positioned to address both Jewish and Gentile believers, forging a bridge between these two diverse groups.

Theological Significance

The heart of Romans is the articulation of the Gospel of Jesus Christ. Paul expounds upon the themes of salvation, grace, faith, righteousness, and the inclusion of both Jews and Gentiles in God's redemptive plan. Central to this is the concept of justification by faith, which underscores that salvation is a gift from God, available to all who believe. The book explores the transformative power of the gospel, highlighting that it is the means through which humanity is reconciled to God and transformed by His indwelling Spirit.

Universal Relevance

While rooted in the context of its time, Romans transcended temporal and cultural boundaries. Its teachings address enduring questions of human existence: the problem of sin, the nature of faith, and the pathway to a right relationship with God. It speaks to the universal human experience, offering hope, redemption, and the promise of a life filled with purpose and meaning.

Moral and Ethical Imperatives

The Book of Romans does not dwell solely on doctrinal matters. It also offers practical guidance on living a life pleasing to God. It imparts wisdom on how to relate to fellow believers, interact with authorities, and demonstrate love and mercy in a broken world. Romans is as much a call to righteous living as it is an exposition of theological truths.

Contemporary Relevance

Two millennia have passed since Romans was written, yet its message remains strikingly contemporary. It speaks to the complexities of the modern world, addressing issues of faith, righteousness, and moral conduct. In a world marked by division and strife, the message of unity and reconciliation in Christ is as relevant as ever.

Embarking on a Journey

As we embark on this journey through the Book of Romans, we invite you to open your heart and mind to the transformative power of the gospel. May these pages inspire you, challenge you, and lead you to a deeper understanding of God's incredible love and grace. The Book of Romans is not just a historical relic; it is a living testament to the enduring power of faith and the redemptive work of Jesus Christ. We hope you find in its verses the answers to life's most profound questions and the hope that transcends all circumstances.

CHAPTER 1
Introduction and Paul's Eagerness to Preach the Gospel

Romans 1:1-7: Introduction and Greeting

Verse 1

- "Paul, a servant of Jesus Christ, called to be an apostle, separated unto the gospel of God,"

Commentary: In this opening verse, Paul identifies himself as a servant of Jesus Christ, emphasizing his role as an apostle, one who is specially called and set apart for a specific mission. He defines his mission as being "separated unto the gospel of God," signifying that his life is dedicated to spreading the message of God through Jesus Christ.

Verse 2

- "Which he had promised afore by his prophets in the holy scriptures,"

Commentary: Paul underscores the continuity between the message he is proclaiming and the promises made by God through the prophets in the holy scriptures of the Old Testament. The gospel is not a new invention but the fulfillment of ancient promises.

Verse 3

- "Concerning his Son Jesus Christ our Lord, which was made of the seed of David according to the flesh;"

Commentary: Here, Paul introduces the central figure of the gospel message, Jesus Christ. He emphasizes that Jesus, in His earthly existence, descended from the lineage of David, thus fulfilling Messianic prophecies that the Messiah would be a descendant of David.

Verse 4

- "And declared to be the Son of God with power, according to the spirit of holiness, by the resurrection from the dead:"

Commentary: Paul highlights a critical aspect of Jesus' identity and authority: He is declared to be the Son of God with power through His resurrection from the dead. This resurrection is the ultimate proof of His divinity and authority.

Verse 5

- "By whom we have received grace and apostleship, for obedience to the faith among all nations, for his name:"

Commentary: Paul speaks of the grace and apostleship he has received through Jesus Christ. His mission, and that of other apostles, is to bring about obedience to the faith among all nations. The purpose of their work is to lead people to faith in Christ.

Verse 6

- "Among whom are ye also the called of Jesus Christ:"

Commentary: Paul addresses the Romans, reminding them that they are among the "called of Jesus Christ." This implies that their faith is not a result of their own efforts but is a divine calling by Jesus Christ.

Verse 7

- "To all that be in Rome, beloved of God, called to be saints: Grace to you and peace from God our Father and the Lord Jesus Christ."

Commentary: Paul's greeting to the Roman Christians reflects the sense of community and belonging among believers. He refers to them as "beloved of God" and "called to be saints." He extends his wishes for grace and peace, invoking God the Father and the Lord Jesus Christ, emphasizing the divine source of these blessings.

In these opening verses of Romans, Paul establishes the foundation for his letter. He introduces himself as an apostle with a special mission to proclaim the gospel of God, centered on Jesus Christ. He emphasizes the continuity between the Old Testament prophecies and the gospel message. Furthermore, he addresses the Roman Christians, reminding them of their divine calling and invoking God's grace and peace upon them. This sets the stage for the profound theological and doctrinal exploration that follows in the rest of the book.

Romans 1:8-15: Paul's Desire to Visit and Preach in Rome

Verse 8

- "First, I thank my God through Jesus Christ for you all, that your faith is spoken of throughout the whole world."

Commentary: Paul begins by expressing gratitude to God through Jesus Christ for the Roman Christians. He commends their faith, highlighting that it is well-known throughout the world. This acknowledgment demonstrates the reputation of the Roman church for its faith and commitment to Christ.

Verse 9

- "For God is my witness, whom I serve with my spirit in the gospel of his Son, that without ceasing I make mention of you always in my prayers;"

Commentary: Paul emphasizes the sincerity of his service to God in the gospel of Jesus Christ. He assures the Romans that he consistently prays for them, highlighting the depth of his concern and affection for this congregation.

Verse 10

- "Making request, if by any means now at length I might have a prosperous journey by the will of God to come unto you."

Commentary: Paul expresses his earnest desire to visit the Roman Christians, seeking a "prosperous journey" according to God's will. His intent is not driven by mere personal interest but by a mission to strengthen and encourage the believers in Rome.

Verse 11

- "For I long to see you, that I may impart unto you some spiritual gift, to the end ye may be established;"

Commentary: Paul reveals his longing to meet the Roman Christians, not just for personal reasons but to impart spiritual gifts to them. He desires their spiritual growth and stability. This reflects the apostle's pastoral care for the faith of the Roman believers.

Verse 12

- "That is, that I may be comforted together with you by the mutual faith both of you and me."

Commentary: Paul emphasizes the mutual encouragement and comfort that would come from his visit to Rome. He sees it as a two-way exchange, where both he and the Roman Christians would be strengthened in faith through their interactions.

Verse 13

- "Now I would not have you ignorant, brethren, that oftentimes I purposed to come unto you, but was let hitherto, that I might have some fruit among you also, even as among other Gentiles."

Commentary: Paul wants the Roman Christians to be aware of his prior intentions to visit them. He explains that various hindrances prevented his visit until that point. His purpose in coming to Rome is to see spiritual fruit, just as he has seen among other Gentile communities, emphasizing the importance of Rome in his ministry.

Verse 14

- "I am debtor both to the Greeks, and to the Barbarians; both to the wise, and to the unwise."

Commentary: Paul asserts that he sees himself as a debtor to all people, regardless of their cultural or intellectual backgrounds. His obligation is to share the gospel with both the educated and the uneducated, highlighting the universal nature of his mission.

Verse 15

- "So, as much as in me is, I am ready to preach the gospel to you that are at Rome also."

Commentary: Paul concludes this section by declaring his readiness and eagerness to preach the gospel in Rome. He is prepared to fulfill his calling and mission by bringing the message of Christ to the believers in the capital city.

In these verses, Paul conveys his deep gratitude for the faith of the Roman Christians and his earnest desire to visit them. He emphasizes the mutual spiritual benefit that would come from their meeting and underscores his commitment to sharing the gospel with all people, whether Greeks or Barbarians, wise or unwise. This section sets the stage for Paul's theological exploration and teaching in the Book of Romans, emphasizing the importance of faith and the universality of the gospel message.

Romans 1:16-17: The Power of the Gospel Revealed

Verse 16

- "For I am not ashamed of the gospel of Christ: for it is the power of God unto salvation to everyone that believeth; to the Jew first, and also to the Greek."

Commentary: In these powerful verses, Paul begins by declaring that he is not ashamed of the gospel of Christ. This statement signifies his unapologetic commitment to preaching and sharing the message of Jesus. He sees the gospel as "the power of God unto salvation." This means that the gospel is not merely good news but is the divine means by which God saves humanity. It is the instrument through which people come to experience salvation. Paul emphasizes the universality of the gospel, stating that it is available "to everyone that believeth." The gospel is not limited by ethnicity or background; it is for all who place their faith in Christ. Paul highlights its inclusivity by mentioning that it is for "the Jew first, and also to the Greek." This reflects the historical progression of the gospel message from its Jewish origins to its broader application to all nations and peoples.

Verse 17

- "For therein is the righteousness of God revealed from faith to faith: as it is written, The just shall live by faith."

Commentary: In this verse, Paul delves into the heart of the gospel message. He explains that in the gospel, the righteousness of God is revealed. This righteousness is not merely a human striving for moral goodness but is God's righteousness, which is imputed to believers through faith in Jesus Christ. It is a righteousness that is given as a gift to those who believe. Paul cites an Old Testament passage from Habakkuk 2:4, saying, "The just shall live by faith." This phrase emphasizes that righteousness and life come through faith in God, not through one's own efforts or works. It underscores the idea that faith is the means by which people are made right with God and find true life.

These verses in Romans 1:16-17 are foundational to the entire letter. They highlight the transformative and inclusive power of the gospel, which brings salvation to all who believe, both Jews and Gentiles. The righteousness of God, received by faith, is the central theme that Paul will explore further in the letter, explaining how it justifies and transforms those who trust in Christ.

Romans 1:18-23: The Wrath of God against Unrighteousness

Verse 18

- "For the wrath of God is revealed from heaven against all ungodliness and unrighteousness of men, who hold the truth in unrighteousness;"

Commentary: In this verse, Paul introduces a critical theme in the letter: the wrath of God. He states that the wrath of God is being revealed from heaven against ungodliness and unrighteousness. This wrath is a response to human sin and rebellion against God. Importantly, Paul mentions that those who "hold the truth in unrighteousness" are subject to this wrath. This suggests that people who possess knowledge of the truth but reject or distort it for unrighteous purposes are accountable to God's judgment.

Verse 19

- "Because that which may be known of God is manifest in them; for God hath shewed it unto them."

Commentary: Paul explains that the reason for this divine judgment is that the knowledge of God is evident within human beings. God has revealed Himself to humanity through creation and the moral conscience. In other words, people have an innate awareness of God's existence and some understanding of His moral standards. This makes them accountable for their actions and decisions.

Verse 20

- "For the invisible things of him from the creation of the world are clearly seen, being understood by the things that are made, even his eternal power and Godhead; so that they are without excuse:"

Commentary: Paul underscores that the evidence of God's existence and attributes is apparent in the created world. Even though God Himself is invisible, His eternal power and divine nature can be clearly perceived through His handiwork in the natural world. Consequently, people have no excuse for denying His existence or the knowledge of His divine attributes.

Verse 21

- "Because that, when they knew God, they glorified him not as God, neither were thankful; but became vain in their imaginations, and their foolish heart was darkened."

Commentary: This verse explains the process of human rebellion against God. People, when they had some knowledge of God, failed to honor Him or express gratitude for His existence. Instead, they turned to idolatry and allowed their thoughts to become futile and their hearts to be darkened. The rejection of God's truth led to moral and spiritual decay.

Verse 22

- "Professing themselves to be wise, they became fools,"

Commentary: Those who turned away from the truth of God's existence and authority, while embracing idolatry, considered themselves wise. In their self-assured wisdom, they actually became foolish. This is a warning against human arrogance and pride that leads to spiritual blindness.

Verse 23

- "And changed the glory of the uncorruptible God into an image made like to corruptible man, and to birds, and four-footed beasts, and creeping things."

Commentary: This verse describes the tragic consequence of human rebellion: the exchange of the glory of the incorruptible God for idolatrous images resembling created things. Instead of worshipping the one true God, they turned to the worship of idols in the form of humans, birds, animals, and even reptiles. This shift from the Creator to created things represents the core of idolatry and symbolizes the moral decline that can result from rejecting God.

In these verses, Paul lays the groundwork for his discussion of human sin and God's righteous judgment. He emphasizes that all people have a basic knowledge of God through creation and conscience, and those who reject this knowledge are held accountable.

The progression from knowledge of God to idolatry and moral degradation serves as a cautionary tale about the consequences of rejecting the truth. These verses underscore the seriousness of human sin and the need for God's redemptive intervention.

Romans 1:24-25: Consequences of Idolatry

Verse 24

- "Wherefore God also gave them up to uncleanness through the lusts of their own hearts, to dishonor their own bodies between themselves:"

Commentary: In this verse, Paul continues to describe the consequences of human rebellion and idolatry. He explains that "God also gave them up" to uncleanness. This means that God allowed people to follow the sinful desires of their own hearts, which led to dishonoring their bodies through immoral practices. The idea here is that God withdrew His protective restraint, allowing people to experience the consequences of their choices.

Verse 25

- "Who changed the truth of God into a lie, and worshipped and served the creature more than the Creator, who is blessed forever. Amen."

Commentary: Here, Paul highlights the fundamental error of idolatry. People exchanged the truth of God for a lie by worshipping created things instead of the Creator. This shift from worshiping the Creator to worshiping what is created is at the core of idolatry. Paul underscores that the Creator is to be blessed forever, emphasizing the eternal nature of God's glory and goodness.

These verses emphasize the downward spiral that can result from idolatry and a rejection of the knowledge of the one true God. When people turn to worship created things or indulge in immoral behavior, they experience the consequences of their choices. Paul's words serve as a warning about the dangers of forsaking God and pursuing idolatry and sinful desires.

Romans 1:26-27: Consequences of Sexual Immorality

Verse 26

- "For this cause, God gave them up unto vile affections: for even their women did change the natural use into that which is against nature:"

Commentary: In this verse, Paul continues to describe the consequences of human rebellion and idolatry. He explains that God gave people up to "vile affections" or shameful passions as a result of their persistent rejection of Him. Paul specifically mentions women who changed natural sexual relations into those who are against nature. This refers to sexual immorality and the distortion of God's intended design for human relationships.

Verse 27

- "And likewise, also the men, leaving the natural use of the woman, burned in their lust one toward another; men with men working that which is unseemly, and receiving in themselves that recompense of their error which was meet."

Commentary: In this verse, Paul addresses both men and women. He describes men who abandoned natural sexual relations with women and, instead, were consumed by lust for other men. The result was engaging in behavior that is considered "unseemly" or morally inappropriate. Paul suggests that these actions lead to a natural consequence or "recompense" for their error.

These verses are often cited in discussions about sexual ethics and homosexuality. Paul's emphasis is on the consequences of sexual immorality, particularly the distortion of God's intended design for human relationships. He underscores that these behaviors are a result of humanity turning away from God, and as a consequence, they experience the negative effects of their choices. Paul's broader message is to highlight the need for repentance and restoration through faith in Christ, as he will later expound in the letter.

Romans 1:28-32: Consequences of a Depraved Mind

Verse 28

- "And even as they did not like to retain God in their knowledge, God gave them over to a reprobate mind, to do those things which are not convenient;"

Commentary: In this verse, Paul highlights the continuing consequences of human rebellion. People, instead of acknowledging and retaining the knowledge of God, deliberately rejected Him. As a result, God gave them over to a "reprobate mind." A reprobate mind is one that has lost its moral compass and discernment. This results in people doing things that are not appropriate or "convenient."

Verse 29

- "Being filled with all unrighteousness, fornication, wickedness, covetousness, maliciousness; full of envy, murder, debate, deceit, malignity; whisperers,"

Commentary: Paul lists a series of sinful behaviors that result from a reprobate mind. These include unrighteousness (moral wrongdoing), fornication (sexual immorality), wickedness (evil conduct), covetousness (greed), maliciousness (ill will), envy (jealousy), murder, debate (contention), deceit (dishonesty), malignity (spitefulness), and whisperers (gossipers). These behaviors illustrate the moral degradation that can occur when people reject God's authority.

Verse 30

- "Backbiters, haters of God, despiteful, proud, boasters, inventors of evil things, disobedient to parents,"

Commentary: Paul continues the list of sinful attributes resulting from a reprobate mind. These include backbiting (slandering), hatred of God, spiteful behavior, pride, boasting, inventing evil things (devising wicked plans), and disobedience to parents. These characteristics reflect the disordered and sinful nature of humanity that has turned away from God.

Verse 31

- "Without understanding, covenant breakers, without natural affection, implacable, unmerciful:"

Commentary: This verse further describes the state of those with a reprobate mind. They lack understanding, break covenants (unfaithful to promises), lack natural affection (showing no genuine love or care), are implacable (unwilling to be reconciled), and are unmerciful (lacking compassion).

Verse 32

- "Who knowing the judgment of God, that they which commit such things are worthy of death, not only do the same, but have pleasure in them that do them."

Commentary: Paul concludes by emphasizing that those who engage in these sinful behaviors are aware of God's righteous judgment. They know that those who practice such things are deserving of death, both in a moral and spiritual sense. However, they not only engage in these sins themselves but also take pleasure in others who do the same. This compounds their guilt and reveals the depth of their moral depravity.

In these verses, Paul presents a stark picture of the consequences of rejecting God and embracing a reprobate mind. The list of sinful behaviors underscores the depth of moral degradation that can result when humanity turns away from God's moral standards. The passage serves as a call to recognize the need for redemption through faith in Christ, who provides a way to be reconciled with God and transformed from a depraved state to one of righteousness.

CHAPTER 2
God's Righteous Judgment and the Role of the Law

Romans 2:1-9: God's Righteous Judgment

Verse 1

- "Therefore thou art inexcusable, O man, whosoever thou art that judgest: for wherein thou judgest another, thou condemnest thyself; for thou that judgest doest the same things."

Commentary: Paul begins this section with a stern admonition against hypocrisy in judgment. He points out that anyone who judges another is inexcusable because, in doing so, they often condemn themselves, as they themselves commit similar sins. This highlights the importance of humility and self-examination when assessing the actions of others.

Verse 2

- "But we are sure that the judgment of God is according to truth against them which commit such things."

Commentary: Paul clarifies that God's judgment is based on truth and righteousness. Unlike human judgment, which can be flawed, God's judgment is perfect and just. He emphasizes that God will judge those who commit sinful deeds accurately and fairly.

Verse 3

- "And thinkest thou this, O man, that judgest them which do such things, and doest the same, that thou shalt escape the judgment of God?"

Commentary: Paul continues to challenge the hypocrisy of judgmental individuals. He asks if they truly believe they can escape God's judgment when they themselves commit similar sins. This question is a call to self-reflection and recognition of the need for God's grace.

Verse 4

- "Or despisest thou the riches of his goodness and forbearance and longsuffering; not knowing that the goodness of God leadeth thee to repentance?"

Commentary: Paul highlights the riches of God's goodness, forbearance, and longsuffering. He reminds readers that God's patience and kindness are intended to lead people to repentance. God's grace provides an opportunity for individuals to turn from their sinful ways and seek reconciliation with Him.

Verse 5

- "But after thy hardness and impenitent heart treasurest up unto thyself wrath against the day of wrath and revelation of the righteous judgment of God;"

Commentary: Paul warns that those who harden their hearts and refuse to repent are, in fact, storing up God's wrath for themselves.

This stored wrath will be revealed on the day of judgment when God's righteous judgment will be unveiled.

Verse 6

- "Who will render to every man according to his deeds:"

Commentary: Paul emphasizes the principle of divine justice. God will render to every individual according to their deeds. This underscores the idea that God's judgment is equitable and just. Each person's actions will have consequences.

Verse 7

- "To them who by patient continuance in well doing seek for glory and honour and immortality, eternal life:"

Commentary: Paul introduces the concept that those who persistently engage in righteous living, seeking glory, honor, and immortality, will be rewarded with eternal life. This emphasizes the importance of a faithful and virtuous life that aligns with God's will.

Verse 8

- "But unto them that are contentious, and do not obey the truth, but obey unrighteousness, indignation and wrath,"

Commentary: Those who are contentious, resistant to the truth, and follow unrighteousness will face indignation and wrath from God. These consequences are the result of persisting in sinful behavior and rejecting the truth.

Verse 9

- "Tribulation and anguish, upon every soul of man that doeth evil, of the Jew first, and also of the Gentile;"

Commentary: Paul concludes by highlighting that tribulation and anguish await every soul that engages in evil actions. This applies not only to Gentiles but also to Jews, underscoring that God's judgment is impartial and universal.

In these verses, Paul addresses the issue of judgment, exposing the dangers of hypocrisy and emphasizing the impartiality of God's judgment. He underscores the need for true repentance and the consequences of unrepentant, sinful behavior. These verses serve as a reminder of the importance of a sincere and obedient heart in the face of God's righteous judgment.

Romans 2:10-19: Judgment and the Law

Verse 10

- "But glory, honour, and peace, to every man that worketh good, to the Jew first, and also to the Gentile:"

Commentary: In this verse, Paul emphasizes that God's judgment is impartial. Both Jews and Gentiles will be rewarded with glory, honor, and peace if they do good. This underscores the idea that God does not show partiality based on one's ethnicity or background. Righteous living is the basis for receiving these rewards.

Verse 11

- "For there is no respect of persons with God."

Commentary: Paul reiterates the impartiality of God's judgment. God does not show favoritism or partiality toward any individual or group based on their status, ethnicity, or any external factors. His judgment is based on righteousness and moral conduct.

Verse 12

- "For as many as have sinned without law shall also perish without law: and as many as have sinned in the law shall be judged by the law;"

Commentary: Here, Paul introduces the concept of law and judgment. He distinguishes between those who sinned without having the Mosaic Law (Gentiles) and those who sinned while under the law (Jews). The idea is that sin incurs judgment, whether or not one had direct knowledge of the Mosaic Law. The specific law by which someone is judged will vary.

Verse 13

- "(For not the hearers of the law are just before God, but the doers of the law shall be justified."

Commentary: Paul emphasizes that merely hearing or knowing the law is not enough to make someone righteous in God's eyes. Instead, it is the doers of the law, those who live in accordance with its moral principles, who will be justified. This underscores the importance of living out one's faith through righteous actions.

Verse 14

- "For when the Gentiles, which have not the law, do by nature the things contained in the law, these, having not the law, are a law unto themselves:"

Commentary: Paul points out that some Gentiles, despite not having the Mosaic Law, naturally behave in ways that align with the moral principles found in the law. These individuals, though lacking the written law, are a "law unto themselves" in the sense that their moral conscience guides their behavior.

Verse 15

- "Which shew the work of the law written in their hearts, their conscience also bearing witness, and their thoughts the mean while accusing or else excusing one another;)"

Commentary: Paul continues to explain that the Gentiles who act in accordance with the moral principles of the law demonstrate that the work of the law is written on their hearts. Their conscience acts as a witness, either accusing them when they do wrong or excusing them when they do right. This highlights the universality of moral awareness and the role of conscience in guiding behavior.

Verse 16

- "In the day when God shall judge the secrets of men by Jesus Christ according to my gospel."

Commentary: Paul reminds his readers that, ultimately, God will judge the secrets of people's hearts. This judgment will occur through Jesus Christ and will be in line with the gospel message that Paul preaches. It underscores the significance of faith in Christ as the basis for God's righteous judgment.

Verse 17

- "Behold, thou art called a Jew, and restest in the law, and makest thy boast of God,"

Commentary: Paul shifts his focus to the Jews, highlighting that they take pride in their identity as Jews, their possession of the law, and their relationship with God. The use of the law as a point of pride will become a central theme in Romans.

Verse 18

- "And knowest his will, and approvest the things that are more excellent, being instructed out of the law;"

Commentary: Paul acknowledges that the Jews possess knowledge of God's will and have been instructed through the law, enabling them to discern what is excellent and morally upright. Their familiarity with the law gives them a significant advantage in understanding God's expectations.

Verse 19

- "And art confident that thou thyself art a guide of the blind, a light of them which are in darkness,"

Commentary: Paul continues to describe the attitude of the Jews, emphasizing their confidence in their role as guides to the morally blind and as lights to those in spiritual darkness. This reflects their sense of responsibility as God's chosen people and custodians of His truth.

In these verses, Paul addresses the themes of impartiality in God's judgment, the relationship between law and righteousness, and the moral awareness present in Gentiles apart from the written law. He also introduces the concept of conscience and underscores the role of faith in Christ as the basis for God's righteous judgment. The passage sets the stage for Paul's deeper exploration of the law, righteousness, and faith in the subsequent chapters of Romans.

Romans 2:20-29: Circumcision of the Heart

Verse 20

- "An instructor of the foolish, a teacher of babes, which hast the form of knowledge and of the truth in the law."

Commentary: In this verse, Paul describes a person who takes on the role of a teacher and guide to others, particularly those who are inexperienced or less knowledgeable. This individual possesses a form of knowledge and truth in the law, suggesting an understanding of God's commandments and moral principles.

Verse 21

- "Thou, therefore, which teachest another, teachest thou not thyself? thou that preachest a man should not steal, dost thou steal?"

Commentary: Paul challenges the hypocrisy of those who teach others but fail to follow their own teachings. He points out that if one teaches against stealing but engages in theft, they are living in contradiction to their own moral instruction.

Verse 22

- "Thou that sayest a man should not commit adultery, dost thou commit adultery? thou that abhorrest idols, dost thou commit sacrilege?"

Commentary: Paul continues to highlight the inconsistency between teaching against certain sins and committing those very sins. He mentions the commandment against adultery and the prohibition of idolatry, emphasizing that these teachers should live in accordance with their own teachings.

Verse 23

- "Thou that makest thy boast of the law, through breaking the law dishonourest thou God?"

Commentary: Paul points out that boasting in the possession of the law while breaking it through one's actions amounts to dishonoring God. The law, when broken by those who claim to uphold it, brings disrepute to God's name and moral standards.

Verse 24

- "For the name of God is blasphemed among the Gentiles through you, as it is written."

Commentary: Paul warns that the actions of those who profess to follow the law but do not live according to its precepts lead to the blaspheming of God's name among the Gentiles. The behavior of these individuals undermines the credibility of the faith they profess.

Verse 25

- "For circumcision verily profiteth if thou keep the law: but if thou be a breaker of the law, thy circumcision is made uncircumcision."

Commentary: Paul draws a significant connection between circumcision and keeping the law. Circumcision is a sign of the covenant between God and the Jewish people, but it only holds value if one truly obeys God's commands. If someone circumcised in the flesh breaks the law, their physical circumcision becomes as if it were uncircumcision.

Verse 26

- "Therefore if the uncircumcision keep the righteousness of the law, shall not his uncircumcision be counted for circumcision?"

Commentary: Paul points out that an uncircumcised person who lives righteously according to the law will, in a spiritual sense, be regarded as if they were circumcised. This underscores the importance of heart obedience over external rituals.

Verse 27

- "And shall not uncircumcision which is by nature, if it fulfil the law, judge thee, who by the letter and circumcision dost transgress the law?"

Commentary: Paul raises the question of whether an uncircumcised person who naturally obeys the law will, in essence, stand in judgment of those who have the written law and circumcision but transgress the law. This highlights the righteousness that comes from a genuine obedience to God's moral standards.

Verse 28

- "For he is not a Jew, which is one outwardly; neither is that circumcision, which is outward in the flesh:"

Commentary: Here, Paul reiterates that being a true Jew is not a matter of outward, physical characteristics, such as circumcision. He emphasizes that authentic Judaism and righteousness are not based on external rituals but on the condition of the heart.

Verse 29

- "But he is a Jew, which is one inwardly, and circumcision is that of the heart, in the spirit, and not in the letter; whose praise is not of men, but of God."

Commentary: Paul concludes this passage with a powerful declaration. A true Jew, according to the spiritual understanding of the term, is one whose heart has been circumcised by the Spirit. This inward circumcision represents a transformation of the heart, where a person's obedience is in the spirit and not merely following the letter of the law. Such individuals receive praise from God rather than seeking the approval of men.

In these verses, Paul underscores the importance of true obedience to God's law, which is a matter of the heart, over mere external rituals. He exposes the hypocrisy of those who teach but do not live according to their own teachings. This passage carries profound implications for understanding the relationship between faith, obedience, and the heart's transformation in God's redemptive plan.

CHAPTER 3

All Are Under Sin, Justification by Faith

Romans 3:1-9: The Advantage of Being Jewish

Verse 1

- "What advantage then hath the Jew? or what profit is there of circumcision?"

Commentary: In this verse, Paul anticipates a question that might arise after his discussion on the true nature of being a Jew and circumcision in the previous chapter. He asks what advantage or profit there is in being a Jew and in undergoing the ritual of circumcision.

Verse 2

- "Much every way: chiefly, because that unto them were committed the oracles of God."

Commentary: Paul's response is that being a Jew has many advantages. Chief among them is the fact that the Jewish people were entrusted with the "oracles of God." This refers to the sacred revelations, including the Scriptures and God's covenant, that were given to the Jewish people. The Jews were chosen as the custodians of God's Word and His divine revelation.

Verse 3

- "For what if some did not believe? shall their unbelief make the faith of God without effect?"

Commentary: Paul addresses a potential objection. He acknowledges that not all Jews believed in God's promises or remained faithful. However, he argues that the unbelief of some does not nullify God's faithfulness or render His promises ineffective. God's faithfulness is unwavering, regardless of human unbelief.

Verse 4

- "God forbid: yea, let God be true, but every man a liar; as it is written, That thou mightest be justified in thy sayings, and mightest overcome when thou art judged."

Commentary: Paul strongly rejects the idea that God's faithfulness could be compromised by human unbelief. He quotes from the Old Testament (Psalm 51:4) to emphasize that God is always true and just. Even if every person were to be considered a liar, God's truth and righteousness would still prevail. This underscores the unshakable character of God's faithfulness and justice.

Verse 5

- "But if our unrighteousness commends the righteousness of God, what shall we say? Is God unrighteous who taketh vengeance? (I speak as a man)"

Commentary: Paul raises a rhetorical question. He notes that if human unrighteousness serves to highlight God's righteousness, then one might ask whether God is unjust when He exercises His judgment.

Paul clarifies that he is speaking in a human way, emphasizing that God's righteousness and justice are not compromised.

Verse 6

- "God forbid: for then how shall God judge the world?"

Commentary: Paul emphatically rejects the idea that God could be unrighteous. He argues that if God were unrighteous in His judgments, He would be unfit to judge the world. In other words, God's role as the righteous judge of all humanity is inherent in His character.

Verse 7

- "For if the truth of God hath more abounded through my lie unto his glory; why yet am I also judged as a sinner?"

Commentary: Paul uses a rhetorical example to illustrate his point. He suggests that if God's truth is magnified by human falsehood or sin (for the sake of His glory), why would anyone still be judged as a sinner? The implication is that God's glory is not served by human sin, but rather by His righteousness and truth.

Verse 8

- "And not rather, (as we be slanderously reported, and as some affirm that we say,) Let us do evil, that good may come? whose damnation is just."

Commentary: Paul addresses a false accusation that his teaching might imply that one should do evil in order for good to result. He unequivocally rejects this notion and asserts that those who make such claims face just condemnation. The idea that good can come from evil actions is a distortion of Paul's teachings.

Verse 9

- "What then? are we better than they? No, in no wise: for we have before proved both Jews and Gentiles, that they are all under sin;"

Commentary: Paul concludes this section by affirming that both Jews and Gentiles are under sin. He emphasizes the universal nature of human sinfulness, regardless of ethnicity or religious background. Paul will continue to develop this theme in the following verses, highlighting the need for God's righteousness and salvation for all.

In these verses, Paul addresses the advantages of being Jewish, defends God's faithfulness and justice, and refutes a misconstrued idea that good may result from evil actions. He underscores the universal nature of human sinfulness, setting the stage for his broader message about the need for God's righteousness and salvation for all people, both Jews and Gentiles.

Romans 3:10-19: The Universality of Sin

Verse 10

- "As it is written, There is none righteous, no, not one."

Commentary: Paul begins this passage by quoting from various Old Testament passages (e.g., Psalm 14:1-3; Psalm 53:1-3; Ecclesiastes 7:20) to emphasize the universal condition of humanity. He makes a powerful declaration that there is not a single person who is inherently righteous. Every individual, regardless of their background or beliefs, falls short of God's perfect standard.

Verse 11

- "There is none that understandeth, there is none that seeketh after God."

Commentary: Building upon the previous verse, Paul asserts that no one naturally seeks after God or comprehends His ways. This reflects the spiritual condition of humanity apart from divine intervention. It underscores the fallen nature of humanity and its inability to seek God in its own strength.

Verse 12

- "They are all gone out of the way, they are together become unprofitable; there is none that doeth good, no, not one."

Commentary: Paul continues to emphasize the universality of sin. He declares that all people have strayed from the right path, have become morally worthless, and no one consistently does what is truly good in God's sight. This verse reflects the pervasive influence of sin on human nature.

Verse 13

- "Their throat is an open sepulchre; with their tongues they have used deceit; the poison of asps is under their lips:"

Commentary: In vivid language, Paul describes the sinful nature of humanity. He likens the human throat to an open grave, where death and corruption reside. He points out that people often use their tongues for deceitful purposes, spreading falsehood and harm. The reference to the poison of asps under their lips suggests that the words and speech of humans can be harmful and destructive.

Verse 14

- "Whose mouth is full of cursing and bitterness:"

Commentary: Paul highlights the negative and hurtful aspects of human speech. He notes that many people's mouths are filled with cursing and bitterness, reflecting the broken and sinful state of human communication.

Verse 15

- "Their feet are swift to shed blood:"

Commentary: This verse draws attention to the tendency of humanity to engage in violence and harm. People are quick to resort to violence and bloodshed, indicating the fallen and sinful nature of human actions.

Verse 16

- "Destruction and misery are in their ways:"

Commentary: Paul asserts that a path of destruction and misery characterizes human conduct. This reflects the consequences of sinful choices and actions, ultimately leading to suffering and despair.

Verse 17

- "And the way of peace have they not known:"

Commentary: Paul emphasizes that, left to their own devices, humanity does not naturally know or pursue the way of peace. The absence of peace reflects the disordered and sin-afflicted state of human existence.

Verse 18

- "There is no fear of God before their eyes."

Commentary: In the concluding verse of this passage, Paul underscores a significant issue—the absence of the fear of God. This doesn't mean terror but rather a reverential awe and acknowledgment of God's existence and authority. Without such reverence, people are prone to sin and moral deviation.

In these verses, Paul's message is clear: all people, Jews and Gentiles alike, are inherently sinful and fallen. He uses a series of Old Testament quotations to illustrate the universality of human sinfulness, emphasizing the need for divine grace and redemption. This sets the stage for his exploration of God's righteousness and the provision of salvation through Jesus Christ in the subsequent verses of Romans.

Romans 3:19-25: Justified by Faith through Christ

Verse 19

- "Now we know that what things soever the law saith, it saith to them who are under the law: that every mouth may be stopped, and all the world may become guilty before God."

Commentary: Paul begins by highlighting the purpose of the law. The law, primarily given to the Jews, served to bring conviction of sin. It was intended to stop every mouth from making excuses and to declare all people guilty before God. This emphasizes that no one can claim righteousness through keeping the law alone, as all have sinned.

Verse 20

- "Therefore by the deeds of the law there shall no flesh be justified in his sight: for by the law is the knowledge of sin."

Commentary: Paul reinforces the idea that the law cannot justify anyone in God's sight. The law's primary function is to reveal and define what sin is, not to provide a means of righteousness. It makes people aware of their transgressions and the need for a solution beyond their own efforts.

Verse 21

- "But now the righteousness of God without the law is manifested, being witnessed by the law and the prophets;"

Commentary: In this pivotal verse, Paul introduces a shift in focus. He declares that the righteousness of God, which is apart from the law, has been revealed. This righteousness, although distinct from the law, is not contrary to it; instead, it is witnessed by the law and the prophets. It was foreshadowed in the Old Testament and finds its fulfillment in Christ.

Verse 22

- "Even the righteousness of God which is by faith of Jesus Christ unto all and upon all them that believe: for there is no difference:"

Commentary: Paul makes a profound statement regarding the means of receiving God's righteousness. It is a righteousness that comes through faith in Jesus Christ. It is not limited to a specific group; it is available to all who believe, without distinction. Faith in Christ is the unifying factor that enables all to partake in God's righteousness.

Verse 23

- "For all have sinned, and come short of the glory of God;"

Commentary: Paul restates a fundamental truth: all people, without exception, have sinned and fallen short of God's glory. This verse underlines the universal need for God's righteousness, as no one can attain His glory through their own efforts.

Verse 24

- "Being justified freely by his grace through the redemption that is in Christ Jesus:"

Commentary: Paul introduces the concept of justification. Those who have sinned can be justified, or declared righteous, freely by God's grace. This justification comes through the redemption provided by Christ Jesus. Redemption, in this context, refers to the act of buying back or delivering from sin's bondage.

Verse 25

- "Whom God hath set forth to be a propitiation through faith in his blood, to declare his righteousness for the remission of sins that are past, through the forbearance of God;"

Commentary: Paul explains that God set forth Jesus Christ as a propitiation. A propitiation is a sacrifice that satisfies the demands of justice and turns away God's wrath. This propitiation is accessed through faith in Christ's blood. It serves to declare God's righteousness and enables the forgiveness of sins that occurred in the past. God's patience (forbearance) in the Old Testament period allowed for the eventual provision of this sacrifice in Christ.

In these verses, Paul unfolds a key theme of the Christian message: justification by faith in Jesus Christ. He highlights that the law exposes human sinfulness and the need for a righteousness that comes through faith. This righteousness is offered freely by God's grace and is made accessible through Christ's redemption and the propitiatory nature of His sacrifice. This sets the stage for the profound exploration of faith and God's righteousness in the following chapters of Romans.

Romans 3:26-31: Justification by Faith and the Law's Fulfillment

Verse 26

- "To declare, I say, at this time his righteousness: that he might be just, and the justifier of him which believeth in Jesus."

Commentary: Paul emphasizes the purpose of God's plan: to declare His righteousness. Through the work of Jesus Christ, God's righteousness is revealed. This righteousness is twofold: it demonstrates God's justice, ensuring that sin is not overlooked, and it shows God as the justifier of those who believe in Jesus. Through faith in Christ, believers are declared righteous, and God's justice is upheld.

Verse 27

- "Where is boasting then? It is excluded. By what law? of works? Nay: but by the law of faith."

Commentary: Paul challenges any notion of boasting in one's own righteousness. Boasting is excluded in the realm of justification by faith. No one can claim that they earned or achieved their righteousness through works of the law. Instead, boasting is negated by the "law of faith," which emphasizes that righteousness is received by believing in Christ, not by human effort.

Verse 28

- "Therefore we conclude that a man is justified by faith without the deeds of the law."

Commentary: Paul presents a clear conclusion: a person is justified by faith and not by the works of the law. This is a central doctrine of the Christian faith. Justification is a gift received through faith in Jesus Christ, not through striving to keep the law's requirements.

Verse 29

- "Is he the God of the Jews only? is he not also of the Gentiles? Yes, of the Gentiles also:"

Commentary: Paul addresses an important question regarding God's inclusivity. He emphasizes that God is not the God of the Jews exclusively but is also the God of the Gentiles. His plan of salvation extends to all people, regardless of their ethnicity.

Verse 30

- "Seeing it is one God, which shall justify the circumcision by faith, and uncircumcision through faith."

Commentary: Paul underscores the oneness of God's plan of justification. Whether a person is circumcised (a Jew) or uncircumcised (a Gentile), both are justified by faith. God's method of justification is consistent and applies to all who have faith in Christ.

Verse 31

- "Do we then make void the law through faith? God forbid: yea, we establish the law."

Commentary: Paul anticipates a potential objection to the doctrine of justification by faith. He emphatically rejects the idea that faith nullifies the law. Instead, he affirms that faith in Christ establishes the law. This means that faith upholds the moral standards and principles embedded in the law while providing the means for sinners to be justified.

In these verses, Paul highlights the core principle of justification by faith. He underscores the universal application of this principle, making it clear that it is not exclusive to any particular group but is available to both Jews and Gentiles. Additionally, he addresses concerns about the law, explaining that faith does not undermine it but, in fact, upholds its moral standards. Faith and the law work together in God's redemptive plan.

CHAPTER 4

Abraham's Faith Justified

Romans 4:1-9: Abraham's Faith Justified

Verse 1

- "What shall we say then that Abraham our father, as pertaining to the flesh, hath found?"

Commentary: Paul begins by addressing the central figure of Abraham, often regarded as the father of the Jewish nation. He asks what was discovered or achieved by Abraham in terms of his physical lineage, referring to his physical descent from the Jewish people.

Verse 2

- "For if Abraham were justified by works, he hath whereof to glory; but not before God."

Commentary: Paul introduces the key theme of justification. He points out that if Abraham were justified by his works or deeds, he could boast or glory in his own achievements, but not before God. Justification by works implies a reliance on one's own efforts, and such a position would not be acceptable before God.

Verse 3

- "For what saith the scripture? Abraham believed God, and it was counted unto him for righteousness."

Commentary: Paul appeals to the scriptural account in Genesis 15:6 to make his case. He highlights that Abraham's righteousness was not attained through works but through faith. When Abraham believed God's promise, his faith was counted or imputed to him as righteousness. This sets the precedent for understanding justification by faith rather than works.

Verse 4

- "Now to him that worketh is the reward not reckoned of grace, but of debt."

Commentary: Paul draws a distinction between earning a reward through one's works and receiving it as an act of grace. When one works for something, it becomes a debt owed, not a free gift of grace. The principle of grace is essential in understanding justification by faith.

Verse 5

- "But to him that worketh not, but believeth on him that justifieth the ungodly, his faith is counted for righteousness."

Commentary: Paul underscores the concept that faith and works operate on different principles. In the context of justification, he highlights that the one who does not rely on their works but instead believes in God, who justifies the ungodly, has their faith counted as righteousness. This highlights God's gracious act of justifying those who do not deserve it.

Verse 6

- "Even as David also describeth the blessedness of the man, unto whom God imputeth righteousness without works,"

Commentary: Paul references King David to further illustrate the concept of imputed righteousness. David described the blessedness of the one to whom God imputes righteousness apart from works. This supports Paul's argument that righteousness is not earned through works but is credited to the believer by God's grace.

Verse 7

- "Saying, Blessed are they whose iniquities are forgiven, and whose sins are covered."

Commentary: Paul quotes from Psalm 32:1-2, emphasizing the blessing of having one's sins forgiven and covered. This serves to illustrate the concept of imputed righteousness and how it relates to forgiveness of sins.

Verse 8

- "Blessed is the man to whom the Lord will not impute sin."

Commentary: Paul concludes this section by emphasizing that a blessed person is one to whom the Lord does not impute or account sin. This further underscores the gracious nature of justification and the forgiveness of sins.

In these verses, Paul presents a foundational argument for the doctrine of justification by faith. He uses the examples of Abraham and David to demonstrate that righteousness is imputed or credited to the believer apart from works. This understanding is crucial in distinguishing between human efforts and God's grace in the process of justification. Justification is not something earned through works but received through faith in God's promises and grace.

Romans 4:10-19: Abraham's Faith and the Promise

Verse 10

- "How was it then reckoned? when he was in circumcision, or in uncircumcision? Not in circumcision, but in uncircumcision."

Commentary: Paul continues to explore the relationship between Abraham's faith and righteousness. He raises the question of when Abraham's faith was reckoned as righteousness—whether it was before or after his circumcision. Paul's answer is clear: it was not in circumcision but in uncircumcision. This emphasizes that Abraham's faith-based righteousness predates the sign of circumcision, showing that righteousness comes by faith, not by adherence to religious rituals.

Verse 11

- "And he received the sign of circumcision, a seal of the righteousness of the faith which he had yet being uncircumcised: that he might be the father of all them that believe, though they be not circumcised; that righteousness might be imputed unto them also:"

Commentary: Paul explains the role of circumcision in Abraham's story. Circumcision served as a sign and seal of the righteousness he had by faith while still uncircumcised. It was not the means of his righteousness but a visible confirmation of it. The significance here is that Abraham became the spiritual father of all who believe, even if they are not circumcised. In this way, righteousness is imputed to them as well, emphasizing the universal applicability of faith-based righteousness.

Verse 12

- "And the father of circumcision to them who are not of the circumcision only, but who also walk in the steps of that faith of our father Abraham, which he had being yet uncircumcised."

Commentary: Abraham is not only the father of the circumcised (the Jews) but also of those who walk in the steps of faith, just as he did when he was still uncircumcised. This emphasizes that being a true child of Abraham is not about physical circumcision but about having the same faith that Abraham exhibited.

Verse 13

- "For the promise, that he should be the heir of the world, was not to Abraham, or to his seed, through the law, but through the righteousness of faith."

Commentary: Paul underscores the importance of faith in the fulfillment of the promise given to Abraham. The promise that Abraham and his descendants would inherit the world was not achieved through adherence to the law but through the righteousness that comes by faith. This points to the superiority of faith as the means of receiving God's promises.

Verse 14

- "For if they which are of the law be heirs, faith is made void, and the promise made of none effect:"

Commentary: Paul makes a logical argument that if inheritance were based on law-keeping, then faith would become useless, and the promise would lose its power. The promise is upheld precisely because it is received by faith rather than earned by adherence to the law.

Verse 15

- "Because the law worketh wrath: for where no law is, there is no transgression."

Commentary: Paul highlights the function of the law. The law reveals and condemns transgressions, and it brings the wrath of God upon those who break it. Where there is no law, there is no transgression because transgressions are violations of the law. In contrast, faith operates in a realm where transgressions are forgiven through God's grace.

Verse 16

- "Therefore it is of faith, that it might be by grace; to the end the promise might be sure to all the seed; not to that only which is of the law, but to that also which is of the faith of Abraham; who is the father of us all,"

Commentary: Paul concludes this section by reiterating the importance of faith. The promise is by faith so that it might be by grace. This ensures that the promise is certain and available to all of Abraham's spiritual descendants. This includes both those who are under the law and those who share the faith of Abraham. Abraham, in this sense, becomes the spiritual father of all who believe, regardless of their background.

In these verses, Paul continues to emphasize the centrality of faith in receiving the promise of righteousness and inheritance. He underscores that the promise given to Abraham was realized through faith, not the law, making it universally accessible to all who share Abraham's faith, both Jews and Gentiles. Faith precedes and surpasses external religious rituals like circumcision, pointing to a righteousness that is credited by faith alone.

Romans 4:20-25: Abraham's Strong Faith and Imputed Righteousness

Verse 20

- "He staggered not at the promise of God through unbelief, but was strong in faith, giving glory to God;"

Commentary: Paul highlights Abraham's unwavering faith in God's promise. Abraham did not doubt or waver in unbelief but remained strong in faith. His faith was characterized by giving glory to God, acknowledging God's power and trustworthiness. This verse underscores the importance of unwavering faith in receiving God's promises.

Verse 21

- "And being fully persuaded that, what he had promised, he was able also to perform."

Commentary: Abraham's faith was grounded in his full persuasion that God, who had made the promise, was fully able to bring it to fulfillment. This points to the foundational aspect of faith—trust in God's ability to accomplish what He has promised. Abraham's conviction in God's capability is a model for all believers.

Verse 22

- "And therefore it was imputed to him for righteousness."

Commentary: This verse encapsulates the central theme of imputed righteousness. Because of Abraham's faith and his unshaken trust in God's promise, his faith was credited to him as righteousness. This means that God considered Abraham as righteous on the basis of his faith rather than his works. This serves as a foundational principle for the New Testament teaching of justification by faith.

Verse 23

- "Now it was not written for his sake alone, that it was imputed to him;"

Commentary: Paul emphasizes that the principle of imputed righteousness is not limited to Abraham's case alone. It serves as a broader lesson for all believers, both in his time and in the future. God's imputation of righteousness through faith is applicable to all who share Abraham's unwavering trust in God's promises.

Verse 24

- "But for us also, to whom it shall be imputed, if we believe on him that raised up Jesus our Lord from the dead;"

Commentary: Paul extends the concept to believers in his own time and beyond. Imputed righteousness is not confined to the past but continues to be applicable for those who believe. It is imputed to those who believe in God, particularly in the resurrection of Jesus, who is referred to as "Jesus our Lord."

Verse 25

- "Who was delivered for our offences, and was raised again for our justification."

Commentary: In this pivotal verse, Paul encapsulates the core message of the Christian faith. Jesus was delivered or crucified for our offenses, bearing the penalty for our sins. His death paid the price for our wrongdoing. However, He was also raised from the dead for our justification. His resurrection serves as the declaration of God's acceptance of Christ's sacrifice and the justification of those who put their faith in Him. It is through the resurrection that believers are declared righteous, not by their own efforts but by faith in what Christ accomplished.

These verses in Romans 4 underscore the crucial relationship between faith and righteousness. Abraham's strong faith, grounded in God's promises, serves as a model for all believers. The imputation of righteousness through faith and the significance of Christ's death and resurrection in the process of justification are central themes that underpin the Christian doctrine of salvation. Faith, as demonstrated by Abraham, is the key to receiving God's imputed righteousness and justification.

CHAPTER 5
Benefits of Justification

Romans 5:1-9: The Benefits of Justification

Verse 1

- "Therefore, being justified by faith, we have peace with God through our Lord Jesus Christ:"

Commentary: Paul begins by highlighting the profound impact of justification by faith. Those who are justified, or declared righteous, by faith in Jesus Christ are no longer at enmity with God. They have peace with God. Justification brings reconciliation, removing the barrier of sin and allowing believers to have a harmonious relationship with their Creator.

Verse 2

- "By whom also we have access by faith into this grace wherein we stand, and rejoice in hope of the glory of God."

Commentary: Through Jesus Christ, believers have access to the grace of God by faith. This grace is not only a one-time event but a place where believers continually stand. It is the grace that enables them to rejoice in the hope of experiencing the glory of God. The hope of glory is a confident expectation of sharing in the divine presence and attributes of God.

Verse 3

- "And not only so, but we glory in tribulations also: knowing that tribulation worketh patience;"

Commentary: Paul acknowledges that the Christian journey includes facing tribulations or trials. However, he emphasizes that believers can "glory" or take joy in these trials. This isn't because they enjoy suffering, but because they understand that tribulations can produce valuable character traits. Tribulation leads to the development of patience, which is an essential quality for enduring the challenges of life.

Verse 4

- "And patience, experience; and experience, hope:"

Commentary: The chain of spiritual growth continues. Patience, developed through enduring trials, leads to experience. This experience, in turn, builds hope. As believers navigate trials with patience, they gain a deeper understanding of God's faithfulness and their own ability to endure, which fosters hope in the promises of God.

Verse 5

- "And hope maketh not ashamed; because the love of God is shed abroad in our hearts by the Holy Ghost which is given unto us."

Commentary: The hope that arises from trials and experience is a sure and unwavering hope. It does not lead to shame or disappointment because it is grounded in the love of God. This love is not merely an intellectual understanding but is "shed abroad in our hearts" by the Holy Spirit. The indwelling presence of the Holy Spirit serves as a constant reminder and assurance of God's love, strengthening our hope.

Verse 6

- "For when we were yet without strength, in due time Christ died for the ungodly."

Commentary: Paul reminds believers of the condition they were in before Christ's sacrifice. They were "without strength" or powerless to save themselves. At the right time, in God's perfect plan, Christ died for the ungodly. This underscores the extraordinary nature of God's love, as Christ gave His life for those who were spiritually weak and lost.

Verse 7

- "For scarcely for a righteous man will one die: yet peradventure for a good man some would even dare to die."

Commentary: Paul contrasts human acts of self-sacrifice with God's act of love. In human terms, it's rare for someone to die for a righteous person, and only some might consider it for a good or virtuous person. This emphasizes the unparalleled nature of Christ's sacrifice: He died for the ungodly, showing a love that goes beyond human comprehension.

Verse 8

- "But God commendeth his love toward us, in that, while we were yet sinners, Christ died for us."

Commentary: The pinnacle of God's love is revealed in Christ's death for humanity. God demonstrated or "commended" His love, not when we were righteous or good, but while we were sinners. This act of love surpasses human understanding. It's not that we deserved it, but God's love is rooted in His nature, and it is His initiative that leads to our reconciliation.

Verse 9

- "Much more then, being now justified by his blood, we shall be saved from wrath through him."

Commentary: Paul concludes this section by emphasizing the significance of Christ's blood in justification. Believers, having been justified by Christ's atoning sacrifice, can have confidence that they will be saved from the wrath of God. The blood of Christ serves as the means of both justification and salvation, providing a secure refuge from God's righteous judgment.

In these verses, Paul delves into the benefits of justification by faith. He highlights that justification brings peace with God, access to His grace, and a firm hope in His glory. It leads to a spiritual progression where trials produce patience, experience, and hope. This hope is grounded in God's love, demonstrated through Christ's sacrifice for the ungodly. The section concludes with the assurance that believers, having been justified by Christ's blood, will be saved from God's wrath. The theme of God's love and the security of believers in Christ runs prominently through these verses.

Romans 5:10-15: Reconciliation through Christ's Atonement
Verse 10

- "For if, when we were enemies, we were reconciled to God by the death of his Son, much more, being reconciled, we shall be saved by his life."

Commentary: Paul starts by emphasizing the profound impact of Christ's sacrifice. He notes that when we were God's enemies, separated from Him due to our sin, we were reconciled to God through the death of His Son, Jesus Christ. This act of reconciliation demonstrates God's love and grace. Paul further emphasizes that if we were reconciled to God through Christ's death, how much more will we, having been reconciled, be saved by His life. This means that Christ's resurrection ensures our ongoing salvation and life with God.

Verse 11

- "And not only so, but we also joy in God through our Lord Jesus Christ, by whom we have now received the atonement."

Commentary: Paul points out that not only are we reconciled and saved through Christ, but we also rejoice in God through our Lord Jesus Christ. The reconciliation with God is a source of great joy for believers. Additionally, through Christ, we have received the atonement, which means our sins have been forgiven and our relationship with God has been restored.

Verse 12

- "Wherefore, as by one man sin entered into the world, and death by sin; and so death passed upon all men, for that all have sinned:"

Commentary: Paul shifts to the concept of sin's entrance into the world through Adam. He explains that sin entered the world through one man (Adam), and death came as a consequence of sin. This death, in both a physical and spiritual sense, passed upon all humanity because all have sinned. This verse introduces the idea of universal sin and its consequences.

Verse 13

- "(For until the law, sin was in the world: but sin is not imputed when there is no law."

Commentary: Paul clarifies that sin existed in the world even before the Mosaic law was given. Sin is not imputed or counted as a transgression of the law when there is no law. In this context, Paul is highlighting that while sin was present, it was not recognized as a violation of a specific law until the Mosaic law was given.

Verse 14

- "Nevertheless death reigned from Adam to Moses, even over them that had not sinned after the similitude of Adam's transgression, who is the figure of him that was to come."

Commentary: Paul underscores that despite the absence of a written law between Adam and Moses, death still reigned over humanity. This reign of death extended even to those who did not sin in a way similar to Adam's transgression, as Adam served as a figure or type of the one who was to come, namely, Jesus Christ. This foreshadows Christ's role in bringing redemption and life.

Verse 15

- "But not as the offence, so also is the free gift. For if through the offence of one many be dead, much more the grace of God, and the gift by grace, which is by one man, Jesus Christ, hath abounded unto many."

Commentary: Paul compares Adam's offense with the free gift of God's grace through Jesus Christ. He points out that if many were affected by Adam's sin and faced spiritual death, the grace of God, and the gift through Jesus Christ, which comes by grace, have much more abounded unto many. The grace of God surpasses the effects of sin, offering redemption and eternal life to all who receive it.

In these verses, Paul explores the contrast between Adam's transgression and the free gift of God through Jesus Christ. He highlights the universal impact of sin and death due to Adam's disobedience but emphasizes the greater abundance of God's grace and the gift of reconciliation and life through Jesus. The work of Christ not only restores what was lost through sin but brings even greater blessings to humanity. This passage underscores the significance of Christ's atonement and its power to reconcile and save those who believe.

Romans 5:16-21: The Abundance of Grace and Righteousness through Christ

Verse 16

- "And not as it was by one that sinned, so is the gift: for the judgment was by one to condemnation, but the free gift is of many offences unto justification."

Commentary: Paul continues his comparison between Adam's sin and the gift of grace through Christ. He points out that the result of Adam's sin was condemnation, a single transgression leading to judgment. In contrast, the free gift of grace in Christ covers many offenses and leads to justification. Christ's sacrifice on the cross provides forgiveness for the multitude of sins that humanity has committed.

Verse 17

- "For if by one man's offence death reigned by one; much more they which receive abundance of grace and of the gift of righteousness shall reign in life by one, Jesus Christ."

Commentary: Paul reiterates the contrast between Adam's offense and Christ's gift. Through Adam's sin, death reigned. However, those who receive the abundance of God's grace and the gift of righteousness through faith in Jesus Christ will not be under the reign of death but will "reign in life" through Him. This speaks to the victory and abundant life that believers have in Christ.

Verse 18

- "Therefore as by the offence of one judgment came upon all men to condemnation; even so by the righteousness of one the free gift came upon all men unto justification of life."

Commentary: Paul emphasizes the universal impact of Adam's sin and Christ's righteousness. Through Adam's offense, judgment came upon all humanity, resulting in condemnation. Similarly, through the righteousness of Christ, the free gift of God's grace extends to all, leading to justification and the promise of eternal life. This underscores the inclusivity of God's offer of salvation through faith in Christ.

Verse 19

- "For as by one man's disobedience many were made sinners, so by the obedience of one shall many be made righteous."

Commentary: Paul continues to draw a parallel between Adam and Christ. Through Adam's disobedience, many were made sinners, inheriting a sinful nature and separated from God. However, through the obedience of Christ, many shall be made righteous. Christ's obedience in His sacrificial death on the cross makes it possible for humanity to be declared righteous before God, not because of their own merits but through faith in Him.

Verse 20

- "Moreover the law entered, that the offence might abound. But where sin abounded, grace did much more abound:"

Commentary: Paul introduces the purpose of the Mosaic law. The law was given to reveal the extent of human sin and the abundance of offenses. However, where sin abounded, God's grace abounded even more. This emphasizes the incredible nature of God's grace, which exceeds the power of sin to condemn.

Verse 21

- "That as sin hath reigned unto death, even so might grace reign through righteousness unto eternal life by Jesus Christ our Lord."

Commentary: Paul concludes by summarizing the contrast between sin and grace. Sin had reigned, leading to death. But through the righteousness of Christ, God's grace reigns, bringing about eternal life through Jesus Christ. Believers are no longer under the dominion of sin and death; they are under the reign of God's grace and the promise of eternal life.

In these verses, Paul presents a powerful contrast between the consequences of Adam's sin and the abundance of God's grace through Jesus Christ. The atonement of Christ not only covers individual sins but provides a path to righteousness and eternal life for all who believe. This passage underscores the universal offer of salvation, the victory over sin and death, and the preeminence of God's grace in Christ's work of redemption.

CHAPTER 6
Dead to Sin, Alive in Christ

Romans 6:1-23: Dead to Sin, Alive in Christ

Verse 1

- "What shall we say then? Shall we continue in sin, that grace may abound?"

Commentary: Paul begins by addressing a potential misunderstanding or misinterpretation of the doctrine of grace. He had just discussed the overwhelming grace of God in the previous chapter, and now he raises the question: Should we keep on sinning so that God's grace can be even more evident? In essence, he is refuting the idea that grace is a license for sinful living.

Verse 2

- "God forbid. How shall we, that are dead to sin, live any longer therein?"

Commentary: Paul emphatically rejects the notion that we should continue in sin. He points out that believers are no longer slaves to sin because they have died to it. Through faith in Christ, we have become dead to sin's power and dominion. This signifies a profound change in our relationship with sin, rendering the old way of life incompatible with the new life in Christ.

Verse 3

- "Know ye not, that so many of us as were baptized into Jesus Christ were baptized into his death?"

Commentary: Paul reminds believers of the significance of their baptism. When they were baptized into Jesus Christ, they were also baptized into His death. This is a symbolic identification with Christ in His death, burial, and resurrection. It signifies a break with the old life dominated by sin and an entrance into a new life in Christ.

Verse 4

- "Therefore we are buried with him by baptism into death: that like as Christ was raised up from the dead by the glory of the Father, even so we also should walk in newness of life."

Commentary: Baptism is not only an identification with Christ's death but also a participation in His resurrection. Believers are buried with Christ in baptism, symbolizing the burial of the old self dominated by sin. Just as Christ was raised from the dead by the glory of the Father, believers are raised to walk in a new life. This new life is marked by righteousness, holiness, and a transformed way of living in alignment with Christ's resurrection power.

Verse 5

- "For if we have been planted together in the likeness of his death, we shall be also in the likeness of his resurrection."

Commentary: Paul reinforces the idea that our union with Christ in His death through baptism is intimately connected with our participation in His resurrection. If we have shared in the likeness of His death, we can expect to share in the likeness of His resurrection.

This underscores the inseparable link between dying to sin and being raised to a new life in Christ.

Verse 6

- "Knowing this, that our old man is crucified with him, that the body of sin might be destroyed, that henceforth we should not serve sin."

Commentary: Paul emphasizes the knowledge that believers should possess. The "old man," representing the sinful, self-centered nature, has been crucified with Christ. The purpose of this crucifixion is to destroy the power and dominion of sin in our lives so that we no longer serve sin. This verse underscores the victory of Christ's sacrifice in breaking the hold of sin over the believer.

Verse 7

- "For he that is dead is freed from sin."

Commentary: Paul reiterates the truth that when one has died with Christ to sin, they are freed from its bondage. The power of sin is broken, and the believer is no longer enslaved by it.

Verse 8

- "Now if we be dead with Christ, we believe that we shall also live with him."

Commentary: Paul emphasizes that if we have died with Christ, we can confidently believe that we will also live with Him. This living with Christ involves both the present reality of our new life in Him and the future hope of eternal life with Him.

Verse 9

- "Knowing that Christ being raised from the dead dieth no more; death hath no more dominion over him."

Commentary: Paul underscores the permanence of Christ's resurrection. Christ, once raised from the dead, will never die again. Death no longer has any dominion or power over Him. This is a reminder of the eternal and victorious nature of Christ's resurrection.

Verse 10

- "For in that he died, he died unto sin once: but in that he liveth, he liveth unto God."

Commentary: Christ's death was a one-time event, and it had a specific purpose—dealing with sin. His resurrection, on the other hand, leads to a life lived unto God. This verse emphasizes that Christ's work is complete, and His resurrection life is directed toward God, free from the bondage of sin.

Verse 11

- "Likewise reckon ye also yourselves to be dead indeed unto sin, but alive unto God through Jesus Christ our Lord."

Commentary: Paul calls believers to apply the truth of their identification with Christ's death and resurrection in their daily lives. They are to consider or reckon themselves as dead to sin and alive to God through Jesus Christ. This is a call to live in the reality of their new identity in Christ, yielding to God and rejecting sin's authority.

Verse 12

- "Let not sin therefore reign in your mortal body, that ye should obey it in the lusts thereof."

Commentary: Based on the previous verses, Paul exhorts believers not to allow sin to rule in their physical bodies. He urges them not to obey sinful desires and lusts. The victory over sin achieved through Christ's death and resurrection should translate into a transformed and obedient life.

Verse 13

- "Neither yield ye your members as instruments of unrighteousness unto sin: but yield yourselves unto God, as those that are alive from the dead, and your members as instruments of righteousness unto God."

Commentary: Paul extends the exhortation to avoid yielding one's body to sin as a tool for unrighteousness. Instead, believers are to yield themselves to God as those who have experienced a new life from the dead. Their physical bodies should be used as instruments of righteousness, serving God's purposes and demonstrating the transformation brought about by their faith in Christ.

Verse 14

- "For sin shall not have dominion over you: for ye are not under the law, but under grace."

Commentary: Paul reiterates the victory over sin that believers experience. Sin no longer has dominion or mastery over them. This victory is due to the fact that they are under grace, not under the law. Under the law, sin's power was magnified, but under grace, sin is overcome through faith in Christ. Believers are no longer under the law's condemnation but under the empowering influence of God's grace.

Romans 6:15-23: Slaves to Righteousness

Verse 15

- "What then? shall we sin, because we are not under the law, but under grace? God forbid."

Commentary: Paul revisits the question of whether believers should continue to sin because they are under grace and not under the law. Once again, he emphatically rejects this idea, exclaiming, "God forbid!" Paul makes it clear that grace is not a license for sinful living.

Verse 16

- "Know ye not, that to whom ye yield yourselves servants to obey, his servants ye are to whom ye obey; whether of sin unto death, or of obedience unto righteousness?"

Commentary: Paul underscores a fundamental principle. We become servants or slaves to that which we choose to obey. If we yield ourselves to obey sin, we become slaves to sin, which ultimately leads to spiritual death. On the other hand, if we choose to obey righteousness, we become servants of obedience, which leads to righteousness and eternal life.

Verse 17

- "But God be thanked, that ye were the servants of sin, but ye have obeyed from the heart that form of doctrine which was delivered you."

Commentary: Paul expresses gratitude that the believers in Rome, who were once slaves to sin, have now obeyed the form of doctrine delivered to them. This doctrine likely refers to the teachings about salvation through faith in Christ and the necessity of being freed from the power of sin. Through their obedience to this teaching, they have experienced a change of heart and allegiance.

Verse 18

- "Being then made free from sin, ye became the servants of righteousness."

Commentary: Paul highlights the transformation that occurs through faith in Christ. By being made free from the enslavement of sin, believers become servants of righteousness. They are no longer under sin's dominion but are now dedicated to living in accordance with God's standards of righteousness.

Verse 19

- "I speak after the manner of men because of the infirmity of your flesh: for as ye have yielded your members servants to uncleanness and to iniquity unto iniquity; even so now yield your members servants to righteousness unto holiness."

Commentary: Paul acknowledges the human weakness and the struggle with sin due to the frailty of the flesh. He uses a common human analogy to illustrate his point. Just as they once yielded their physical bodies to uncleanness and sinful behavior, he encourages them to now yield their bodies as servants to righteousness, leading to holiness. The idea is that their physical actions should reflect their new allegiance to Christ.

Verse 20

- "For when ye were the servants of sin, ye were free from righteousness."

Commentary: Paul contrasts the previous state of being servants of sin with the absence of righteousness in that condition. When they were slaves to sin, they were not associated with righteousness. Sin and righteousness are mutually exclusive, and sin's dominance keeps righteousness at bay.

Verse 21

- "What fruit had ye then in those things whereof ye are now ashamed? for the end of those things is death."

Commentary: Paul prompts the believers to reflect on the outcome of their previous sinful lifestyle. He asks what benefits or fruit they obtained from the things they are now ashamed of. The obvious answer is that the end result of those sinful behaviors is death, not only physical but also spiritual death—separation from God.

Verse 22

- "But now being made free from sin, and become servants to God, ye have your fruit unto holiness, and the end everlasting life."

Commentary: Paul contrasts their former state as slaves to sin with their current status of being set free from sin and becoming servants of God. The result of this change is "fruit unto holiness," which signifies a life characterized by holiness and righteous living. The ultimate end of this transformed life is everlasting life, contrasting with the death that sin leads to.

Verse 23

- "For the wages of sin is death; but the gift of God is eternal life through Jesus Christ our Lord."

Commentary: Paul encapsulates the entire message of this passage with a well-known statement. Sin earns wages, and that wage is death, both in the present and in the spiritual sense. However, God offers a gift, which is eternal life, and it is through Jesus Christ our Lord.

This verse beautifully summarizes the gospel message—salvation from the consequence of sin and the gift of eternal life through faith in Christ.

In this passage, Paul emphasizes the transformation that occurs in the lives of believers through faith in Christ. They move from being slaves to sin to becoming servants of righteousness and God. This transformation leads to a life characterized by holiness and ultimately results in the gift of eternal life through Jesus Christ.

CHAPTER 7
The Struggle with Sin

Romans 7:1-9: Released from the Law through Christ

Verse 1

- "Know ye not, brethren, (for I speak to them that know the law,) how that the law hath dominion over a man as long as he liveth?"

Commentary: Paul begins this section by addressing fellow believers, especially those familiar with the Jewish law. He reminds them that the law has authority over a person for as long as they are alive. This is a foundational principle he's about to explain.

Verse 2

- "For the woman which hath an husband is bound by the law to her husband so long as he liveth; but if the husband be dead, she is loosed from the law of her husband."

Commentary: Paul uses a marital analogy to illustrate his point. A married woman is bound by the law to her husband as long as he is alive. This reflects the ongoing authority of the law. If her husband dies, she is no longer bound by that law, and she is free to marry another.

Verse 3

- "So then if, while her husband liveth, she be married to another man, she shall be called an adulteress: but if her husband be dead, she is free from that law; so that she is no adulteress, though she be married to another man."

Commentary: Paul explains the consequences of marrying another man while her husband is alive. This act is considered adultery because she is still bound by the law to her living husband. However, if her husband dies, she is freed from the law and can marry another without committing adultery.

Verse 4

- "Wherefore, my brethren, ye also are become dead to the law by the body of Christ; that ye should be married to another, even to him who is raised from the dead, that we should bring forth fruit unto God."

Commentary: Paul now applies this analogy to believers. He tells them that through Christ's death, they have become "dead to the law." This means that the law's authority over them has ended. They are no longer bound by the law's requirements and penalties. Instead, they are now free to be "married to another," which is a spiritual union with Christ, who has been raised from the dead. This union is for the purpose of bearing fruit for God, living a life that reflects God's righteousness and character.

Verse 5

- "For when we were in the flesh, the motions of sins, which were by the law, did work in our members to bring forth fruit unto death."

Commentary: Paul contrasts the former state of believers "in the flesh" when they were under the dominion of sin and the law. In that state, the sinful inclinations within them, stirred by the law's requirements, led to actions that produced spiritual death. The law, while good and holy, exposed the sin within, but it couldn't save or transform the individual.

Verse 6

- "But now we are delivered from the law, that being dead wherein we were held; that we should serve in newness of spirit, and not in the oldness of the letter."

Commentary: Paul reinforces the idea that believers are now "delivered from the law." They are no longer held captive by its demands and the condemnation it brought. Instead, they serve God in a "newness of spirit," which means they serve with a renewed heart and a transformed nature, guided by the Holy Spirit. Their service is no longer legalistic, focused on the letter of the law, but it's a service of grace and the Spirit.

Verse 7

- "What shall we say then? Is the law sin? God forbid. Nay, I had not known sin, but by the law: for I had not known lust, except the law had said, Thou shalt not covet."

Commentary: Paul anticipates a question or objection that might arise: "Is the law sin?" He emphatically answers, "God forbid." The law itself is not sinful; it is holy and reveals God's righteous standards. Rather, the law's function is to expose and define sin. Paul uses the example of the commandment "Thou shalt not covet" to illustrate how the law makes one aware of sin. The law defines sin by showing where people fall short of God's requirements.

Verse 8

- "But sin, taking occasion by the commandment, wrought in me all manner of concupiscence. For without the law sin was dead."

Commentary: Paul explains that sin seizes the opportunity provided by the law's commandments to produce all sorts of sinful desires (concupiscence) in individuals. In the absence of the law, sin would not have been as clearly recognized as a transgression.

Verse 9

- "For I was alive without the law once: but when the commandment came, sin revived, and I died."

Commentary: Paul reflects on his own experience. He recalls a time when he was "alive without the law" or unaware of the full extent of his sin. However, when the commandment (the law) came, it awakened a consciousness of sin, and he became aware of his sinful state. This awareness led to a spiritual "death," the realization of his separation from God due to sin.

In this passage, Paul addresses the role of the law in the lives of believers. He emphasizes that believers have been released from the law's authority through Christ's death, which has allowed them to be united with Him. He clarifies that the law is not sin but rather reveals sin in human nature. The law defines sin and highlights the need for grace and transformation by the Spirit. This passage underscores the idea that believers now serve God with a transformed heart and are no longer bound by a legalistic approach to righteousness.

Romans 7:10-17: The Struggle with Sin and the Role of the Law

Verse 10

- "And the commandment, which was ordained to life, I found to be unto death."

Commentary: In this verse, Paul continues to reflect on the function of the law. He refers to the commandments as something that was designed to lead to life, intended for the well-being and moral guidance of the people. However, he found that in his experience, the law brought about a realization of his sin and the spiritual death that results from sin. The law, though good, couldn't provide life but rather exposed the sin within him.

Verse 11

- "For sin, taking occasion by the commandment, deceived me, and by it slew me."

Commentary: Paul delves deeper into the relationship between the law and sin. He explains that sin took advantage of the commandments, deceiving him by leading him into sin. The law, by setting clear standards and exposing transgressions, revealed the deceitfulness of sin and the deadly consequences it brings.

Verse 12

- "Wherefore the law is holy, and the commandment holy, and just, and good."

Commentary: Paul takes a moment to reaffirm the holiness, justice, and goodness of the law. He doesn't want his previous comments to be misunderstood as criticism of the law itself. The law, as given by God, is inherently holy and just, providing a righteous standard for human conduct.

Verse 13

- "Was then that which is good made death unto me? God forbid. But sin, that it might appear sin, working death in me by that which is good; that sin by the commandment might become exceeding sinful."

Commentary: Paul addresses a potential misunderstanding. He clarifies that the goodness of the law did not make death come to him. Instead, it was sin that used the goodness of the law to bring about death. The law exposed the true nature and enormity of sin, making sin appear exceedingly sinful. The law magnifies the severity of sin by revealing how far short it falls from God's perfect standards.

Verse 14

- "For we know that the law is spiritual: but I am carnal, sold under sin."

Commentary: Paul acknowledges that the law is spiritual, reflecting God's character and perfect standards. However, he contrasts this with his own state of being "carnal" or of the flesh, which is susceptible to sin. He describes himself as being "sold under sin," illustrating the bondage that sin has over the human condition.

Verse 15

- "For that which I do I allow not: for what I would, that do I not; but what I hate, that do I."

Commentary: Paul confesses the inner struggle he faces as a believer. He expresses the tension between his desires and his actions. There's a discrepancy between what he knows is right and what he actually does. This reflects the universal human struggle with sin and the imperfection of human nature.

Verse 16

- "If then I do that which I would not, I consent unto the law that it is good."

Commentary: Paul acknowledges that when he does what he does not want to do, he, in essence, affirms the goodness of the law. His own frustration and struggle highlight the moral goodness of the law, which sets a righteous standard that he desires to follow.

Verse 17

- "Now then it is no more I that do it, but sin that dwelleth in me."

Commentary: In this verse, Paul draws a distinction between his true self as a redeemed child of God and the indwelling sin that still affects his actions. He is essentially saying that the sinful actions are not a reflection of his true identity in Christ but are the result of the sin that continues to reside within him. This is a key concept in understanding the ongoing battle between the flesh and the spirit that believers experience.

In these verses, Paul continues to explore the relationship between the law and sin. He emphasizes the holiness and goodness of the law while acknowledging the struggle believers face due to the presence of indwelling sin. This passage speaks to the tension between one's desires for righteousness and the ongoing struggle with sin, highlighting the need for God's grace and the transformative work of the Holy Spirit in the life of a believer.

Romans 7:18-25: The Struggle with Sin and the Victory in Christ

Verse 18

- "For I know that in me (that is, in my flesh,) dwelleth no good thing: for to will is present with me; but how to perform that which is good I find not."

Commentary: Paul begins this section by candidly acknowledging the ongoing struggle with sin. He recognizes that within his flesh, there is no inherent goodness. Despite having a desire and a willingness to do what is right, he finds himself unable to consistently carry out the good he desires. This internal conflict is a common experience among believers. It reflects the tension between the regenerate spirit and the fallen human nature.

Verse 19

- "For the good that I would I do not: but the evil which I would not, that I do."

Commentary: Paul continues to describe the inner struggle. He emphasizes that the good he wants to do, he often fails to do. Conversely, the evil he desires to avoid, he sometimes finds himself doing. This internal conflict highlights the imperfection of the human condition and the influence of indwelling sin.

Verse 20

- "Now if I do that I would not, it is no more I that do it, but sin that dwelleth in me."

Commentary: Paul makes a crucial distinction here. He separates his true self, the redeemed inner being, from the sinful actions he sometimes engages in. When he commits actions, he does not want to do, he attributes these actions to the sin dwelling within him, rather than his redeemed self in Christ. This underscores the coexistence of two opposing forces within the believer—the spirit and the flesh.

Verse 21

- "I find then a law, that, when I would do good, evil is present with me."

Commentary: Paul describes a kind of spiritual law at work within him. He recognizes that whenever he wants to do what is good and right, the presence of evil is still there, tempting and influencing him. This acknowledgment emphasizes the ongoing spiritual warfare between the desires of the renewed spirit and the pull of the old sinful nature.

Verse 22

- "For I delight in the law of God after the inward man."

Commentary: Despite the internal struggle, Paul declares his delight in the law of God. He speaks of the inner or inward man, referring to the regenerated, spiritual aspect of himself. This inner self genuinely desires to follow God's law and do what is right.

Verse 23

- "But I see another law in my members, warring against the law of my mind and bringing me into captivity to the law of sin which is in my members."

Commentary: Paul recognizes the conflict within him—the law of sin in his physical members, or his flesh, is in constant opposition to the law of his mind, which seeks to obey God. This war within is a vivid depiction of the ongoing battle between the desires of the regenerated mind and the sinful impulses of the flesh.

Verse 24

- "O wretched man that I am! who shall deliver me from the body of this death?"

Commentary: In a moment of deep self-awareness, Paul exclaims his wretchedness. He keenly feels the weight of this internal struggle with sin. His cry reflects the universal human experience of wrestling with sin's power and the desire for deliverance from it. Paul longs for liberation from the "body of this death," symbolizing the sin-infected mortal body.

Verse 25

- "I thank God through Jesus Christ our Lord. So then with the mind I myself serve the law of God, but with the flesh the law of sin."

Commentary: Paul finds the answer to his cry for deliverance in Jesus Christ, the Lord. He recognizes that it is through Christ that he can find victory over this internal struggle. With his mind, or the inner man, he serves the law of God and desires to obey it. However, with the flesh, he is still subject to the influence of the sinful nature. This verse emphasizes the necessity of relying on Christ and the empowering work of the Holy Spirit to overcome the ongoing battle with sin.

In this passage, Paul provides a profound and honest description of the inner struggle with sin that believers often face. He underscores the tension between the redeemed spirit, which desires to obey God, and the flesh, which is still subject to sin's influence. While the struggle is real, Paul's ultimate hope and deliverance come from Jesus Christ. This passage reminds believers of their ongoing need for dependence on Christ and the sanctifying work of the Holy Spirit. It also offers assurance that victory is found in Christ, even amid the battle with sin.

CHAPTER 8
Life in the Spirit

Romans 8:1-9: Freedom in the Spirit

Verse 1

- "There is, therefore, now no condemnation to them which are in Christ Jesus, who walk not after the flesh, but after the Spirit."

Commentary: In this powerful opening verse, Paul proclaims the freedom that believers have in Christ Jesus. He emphasizes that those who are "in Christ Jesus" are not condemned. This means that their sins are forgiven, and they are no longer under the guilt and punishment of sin. However, a crucial condition is mentioned: they should "walk not after the flesh but after the Spirit." In other words, their conduct should reflect the indwelling presence of the Holy Spirit. This verse underscores the importance of living in obedience to the Spirit.

Verse 2

- "For the law of the Spirit of life in Christ Jesus hath made me free from the law of sin and death."

Commentary: Paul introduces a contrast between two "laws." The first is the "law of the Spirit of life in Christ Jesus." This law represents the transformative power of the Holy Spirit, which brings life and freedom from sin and death. The second is the "law of sin and death," which characterizes the bondage and condemnation that sin brings. Through faith in Christ, believers are liberated from the dominion of sin and death.

Verse 3

- "For what the law could not do, in that it was weak through the flesh, God sending his own Son in the likeness of sinful flesh, and for sin, condemned sin in the flesh."

Commentary: Paul explains that the Mosaic law, while holy and good, was unable to provide the power to overcome sin because of the weakness of human flesh. However, God took action. He sent His Son, Jesus Christ, in human form, "in the likeness of sinful flesh." Jesus came to condemn sin by His sinless life and sacrificial death. He bore the penalty of sin in His own flesh, thereby providing the means for believers to be set free from the power of sin.

Verse 4

- "That the righteousness of the law might be fulfilled in us, who walk not after the flesh, but after the Spirit."

Commentary: The purpose of Christ's redemptive work is that the righteousness required by the law might be realized in believers. It is not fulfilled by legalistic adherence to the law but by those who "walk not after the flesh, but after the Spirit." In other words, it is the Holy Spirit's transformative work in the lives of believers that empowers them to live in accordance with the righteous standards of God's law.

Verse 5

- "For they that are after the flesh do mind the things of the flesh, but they that are after the Spirit the things of the Spirit."

Commentary: Paul distinguishes between two mindsets or orientations. Those who are "after the flesh" focus on the things of the flesh, which are worldly and sinful desires. In contrast, those who are "after the Spirit" prioritize spiritual matters and seek to follow the guidance and empowerment of the Holy Spirit. This verse underscores the importance of one's mindset and priorities in determining their way of life.

Verse 6

- "For to be carnally minded is death, but to be spiritually minded is life and peace."

Commentary: Paul elaborates on the consequences of these different mindsets. To be "carnally minded" or focused on the desires of the flesh results in spiritual death, separation from God. On the other hand, to be "spiritually minded," seeking to follow the guidance of the Holy Spirit, leads to life and peace. This highlights the transformation and inner peace that come from living in alignment with God's Spirit.

Verse 7

- "Because the carnal mind is enmity against God: for it is not subject to the law of God, neither indeed can be."

Commentary: Paul explains why the carnal mind is hostile or at enmity with God. It is because the carnal mind is inherently rebellious and disobedient to the law of God. It cannot submit to God's righteous standards. This verse reinforces the idea that a transformation of the mind and heart is needed to be in harmony with God's will.

Verse 8

- "So then, they that are in the flesh cannot please God."

Commentary: Paul concludes this section by emphasizing that those who live according to the flesh, in rebellion against God's ways, are unable to please God. The unregenerate, untransformed life is inherently incapable of satisfying God's righteous requirements.

Verse 9

- "But ye are not in the flesh, but in the Spirit if so be that the Spirit of God dwell in you. Now, if any man has not the Spirit of Christ, he is none of   his."

Commentary: Paul addresses the believers directly, highlighting their identity and status. He asserts that they are "not in the flesh but in the Spirit" if the Spirit of God dwells in them. This indwelling of the Holy Spirit is a defining characteristic of a true believer. Without the Spirit of Christ, a person does not belong to Christ. This verse underscores the importance of the Holy Spirit's presence as a mark of genuine faith.

In this passage, Paul emphasizes the transformative power of the Holy Spirit and the freedom believers have in Christ Jesus. Through faith in Christ and the indwelling of the Spirit, believers are liberated from the power of sin and death. The contrast between the flesh and the Spirit highlights the importance of having a mindset aligned with God's purposes and priorities. Believers are called to live according to the Spirit, allowing the Spirit's guidance and transformation to lead them in a way that pleases God.

Romans 8:10-19: Heirs with Christ and the Groaning Creation

Verse 10

- "And if Christ be in you, the body is dead because of sin; but the Spirit is life because of righteousness."

Commentary: Paul begins by emphasizing the coexistence of two contrasting realities. The presence of Christ within believers signifies a spiritual life, as the Spirit of God dwells in them. At the same time, their physical bodies are subject to death because of the presence of sin. The Spirit brings life through righteousness, setting the stage for the tension between the temporal and the eternal.

Verse 11

- "But if the Spirit of him that raised up Jesus from the dead dwell in you, he that raised up Christ from the dead shall also quicken your mortal bodies by his Spirit that dwelleth in you."

Commentary: Paul points to the resurrection power of the Holy Spirit. Just as the Spirit raised Jesus from the dead, He will also give life to the mortal bodies of believers. This is a profound statement of the future hope of bodily resurrection for those who have the Spirit dwelling in them. It connects the present spiritual life with the future bodily transformation.

Verse 12

- "Therefore, brethren, we are debtors, not to the flesh, to live after the flesh."

Commentary: Paul transitions to an exhortation. He urges believers to live in the realization of their new spiritual reality. They are not bound or obligated to live according to the flesh and its sinful desires. Rather, they owe their allegiance to the Spirit and are called to live in accordance with His leading.

Verse 13

- "For if ye live after the flesh, ye shall die: but if ye through the Spirit do mortify the deeds of the body, ye shall live."

Commentary: Paul issues a stern warning. Living according to the flesh leads to spiritual death and separation from God. However, by the enabling power of the Spirit, believers are called to put to death the sinful deeds of the body. This act of "mortification" signifies the ongoing process of sanctification, where believers strive to live in obedience to God.

Verse 14

- "For as many as are led by the Spirit of God, they are the sons of God."

Commentary: Paul highlights the defining characteristic of God's children: they are led by the Spirit of God. This leadership is both personal and transformative. Being led by the Spirit is a mark of genuine sonship or adoption into God's family. It involves following the Spirit's guidance in daily life.

Verse 15

- "For ye have not received the spirit of bondage again to fear, but ye have received the Spirit of adoption, whereby we cry, Abba, Father."

Commentary: Paul contrasts the Spirit of God with a spirit of bondage and fear. Believers, through the Spirit, have received the Spirit of adoption. This adoption into God's family means that they can approach God intimately, addressing Him as "Abba, Father." The Spirit enables this close and personal relationship with God.

Verse 16

- "The Spirit itself beareth witness with our spirit that we are the children of God."

Commentary: The Holy Spirit testifies or bears witness with the spirit of believers that they are indeed God's children. This inner assurance and affirmation of one's relationship with God come through the work of the Spirit. It's a deep sense of belonging to God's family.

Verse 17

- "And if children, then heirs; heirs of God and joint-heirs with Christ if so be that we suffer with him, that we may be also glorified together."

Commentary: Paul introduces the concept of inheritance. As children of God, believers are also heirs. They share in the inheritance of God's blessings and, remarkably, are "joint-heirs with Christ." This means that believers participate in the inheritance that belongs to Christ, which includes the promises of eternal life and the Kingdom of God. However, Paul notes the reality of suffering with Christ as part of this joint inheritance. Believers share in both the sufferings and the glory of Christ.

Verse 18

- "For I reckon that the sufferings of this present time are not worthy to be compared with the glory which shall be revealed in us."

Commentary: Paul acknowledges the present sufferings and trials that believers may face. However, he holds a perspective that these sufferings are incomparable to the future glory that will be revealed in believers. This glory refers to the fullness of God's redemptive work, culminating in the resurrection and the new heavens and new earth. It's a message of hope and encouragement in the face of present difficulties.

Verse 19

- "For the earnest expectation of the creature waiteth for the manifestation of the sons of God."

Commentary: Paul introduces a unique perspective on creation's longing. He personifies creation as having an "earnest expectation" and eagerly awaiting the revelation of God's children. Creation itself is seen as groaning in anticipation of the full realization of God's redemptive plan. This imagery emphasizes the cosmic impact of God's work in and through believers.

In these verses, Paul expounds on the profound truths of the believer's relationship with the Holy Spirit, their status as children and heirs of God, and the future glory that awaits them. He also introduces the intriguing concept of creation's longing for the full manifestation of God's children, underscoring the cosmic scope of God's redemptive plan. This passage provides a powerful message of hope, assurance, and encouragement for believers as they navigate the challenges of the present while looking forward to the future glory.

Romans 8:20-29: The Hope of Creation and the Groaning of Believers

Verse 20

- "For the creature was made subject to vanity, not willingly, but by reason of him who hath subjected the same in hope."

Commentary: Paul begins by addressing the condition of creation, which was made "subject to vanity" or futility. This occurred not by the choice of the created order but because of God's design. Importantly, God subjected creation to this state "in hope." This suggests that there is a divine purpose and plan for creation, even in its present state of imperfection. The hope alludes to the future redemption and restoration of the entire created order.

Verse 21

- "Because the creature itself also shall be delivered from the bondage of corruption into the glorious liberty of the children of God."

Commentary: Paul reveals the future destiny of creation. It will be "delivered from the bondage of corruption" or decay. Creation will be set free from its current state of imperfection and decay and will enter into the "glorious liberty" that belongs to the children of God. This liberty refers to the fullness of redemption and transformation.

Verse 22

- "For we know that the whole creation groaneth and travaileth in pain together until now."

Commentary: Paul underscores the present condition of creation—it "groaneth and travaileth in pain." This signifies the brokenness and suffering present in the world. Creation itself is longing for the day of its renewal. The "until now" indicates that this groaning has been a constant reality throughout human history.

Verse 23

- "And not only they, but ourselves also, which have the firstfruits of the Spirit, even we ourselves groan within ourselves, waiting for the adoption, to wit, the redemption of our body."

Commentary: Paul expands the perspective to include believers. He notes that believers, who have already received the "firstfruits of the Spirit," also share in the groaning. This groaning represents their longing for the completion of their redemption—the "adoption" and "redemption of our body." This refers to the future resurrection and glorification of their physical bodies, a key element of their full salvation.

Verse 24

- "For we are saved by hope: but hope that is seen is not hope: for what a man seeth, why doth he yet hope for?"

Commentary: Paul highlights the role of hope in the believer's life. Salvation itself is intricately linked to hope. Hope is most powerful when what is hoped for is not yet seen. If something is already seen or possessed, there is no need for hope. In the context of salvation, believers hope for the fullness of their redemption, which is yet to be fully realized.

Verse 25

- "But if we hope for that we see not, then do we with patience wait for it."

Commentary: Paul emphasizes the patience required in the journey of faith. Believers hope for what they have not yet seen or experienced fully. This hope necessitates a patient waiting, trusting in God's promises and the fulfillment of His redemptive plan.

Verse 26

- "Likewise, the Spirit also helpeth our infirmities: for we know not what we should pray for as we ought: but the Spirit itself maketh intercession for us with groanings which cannot be uttered."

Commentary: Paul introduces the role of the Holy Spirit in helping believers in their weakness. The Spirit comes alongside to assist them, particularly in prayer. At times, believers may not know how to pray effectively, but the Spirit intercedes on their behalf with "groanings which cannot be uttered." This highlights the Spirit's intimate involvement in the believer's spiritual journey.

Verse 27

- "And he that searcheth the hearts knoweth what is the mind of the Spirit, because he maketh intercession for the saints according to the will of God."

Commentary: God, who "searcheth the hearts," knows the mind and intentions of the Holy Spirit's intercession. The Spirit's prayers are perfectly aligned with the will of God. This demonstrates the profound unity between the Spirit and God's purposes, ensuring that the Spirit's intercession is in harmony with God's divine plan.

Verse 28

- "And we know that all things work together for good to them that love God, to them who are the called according to his purpose."

Commentary: Paul provides a well-known and comforting assurance. Believers can have confidence that "all things work together for good" in their lives. This doesn't mean that everything that happens is inherently good but that God, in His sovereignty, works all circumstances for the ultimate good of those who love Him and are called according to His purpose. This verse emphasizes God's providential care over His children.

Verse 29

- "For whom he did foreknow, he also did predestinate to be conformed to the image of his Son, that he might be the firstborn among many brethren."

Commentary: Paul concludes this section with a reference to God's foreknowledge and predestination. Those whom God foreknew, He also predestined to a specific purpose: to be "conformed to the image of his Son." This predestination is not about determining who will be saved but about God's plan to transform believers into Christlikeness. It is a process of spiritual growth and sanctification, with the ultimate goal of glorifying Christ and having Him as the "firstborn among many brethren."

In these verses, Paul explores the relationship between believers, creation, and the Holy Spirit in the context of hope and future redemption. He highlights the groaning and longing of both creation and believers for the fulfillment of God's redemptive plan. The Holy Spirit plays a significant role in intercession, and believers are assured that God is working all things for their good, ultimately leading to their conformity to the image of Christ.

Romans 8:30-39: The Unbreakable Love of God

Verse 30

- "Moreover whom he did predestinate, them he also called: and whom he called, them he also justified: and whom he justified, them he also glorified."

Commentary: Paul continues his discussion on God's divine plan. He presents a sequence of events that are part of God's redemptive purpose.

- Predestination: Before the foundation of the world, God chose and predestined certain individuals for salvation.

- Calling: Those whom God predestined, He called to Himself. This is the effectual call of God, drawing them into a relationship with Him.

- Justification: Those who responded to the call in faith were justified. Justification is the legal declaration of righteousness in Christ.

- Glorification: In God's perspective, it is so certain that those whom He justified will also be glorified. Glorification refers to the future transformation of believers into the likeness of Christ.

This verse illustrates the unbroken chain of God's grace, emphasizing the security of believers in His redemptive plan.

Verse 31

- "What shall we then say to these things? If God be for us, who can be against us?"

Commentary: Paul invites contemplation on the significance of God's redemptive work. He rhetorically asks, "If God is for us, who can be against us?" This statement underscores the idea that God's favor and protection are more powerful than any opposition or challenge believers may face. It conveys a message of confidence and assurance in God's sovereignty.

Verse 32

- "He that spared not his own Son, but delivered him up for us all, how shall he not with him also freely give us all things?"

Commentary: Paul highlights the greatest act of God's love and provision: the sacrifice of His own Son, Jesus Christ, for the salvation of humanity. The logic is clear—God, who gave His most precious gift (His Son), will undoubtedly provide everything necessary for the well-being and spiritual growth of believers. This verse underscores the idea of God's abundant grace and care.

Verse 33

- "Who shall lay anything to the charge of God's elect? It is God that justifieth."

Commentary: Paul emphasizes the security of those whom God has chosen (His elect). No one can successfully bring charges against them because it is God who justifies. This underscores the divine authority and finality of God's declaration of righteousness for believers.

Verse 34

- "Who is he that condemneth? It is Christ that died, yea rather, that is risen again, who is even at the right hand of God, who also maketh intercession for us."

Commentary: Paul raises a rhetorical question: Who can condemn believers? He asserts that no one can condemn because Christ, who died for their sins and was raised from the dead, is now seated at the right hand of God. Furthermore, Christ continually intercedes for believers, serving as their Advocate and High Priest before God. This provides believers with confidence in their eternal security.

Verse 35

- "Who shall separate us from the love of Christ? Shall tribulation, or distress, or persecution, or famine, or nakedness, or peril, or sword?"

Commentary: Paul introduces a series of challenges and hardships that believers might face. He asks whether any of these difficulties can separate believers from the love of Christ. The implied answer is that none of these external circumstances can sever the bond between Christ's love and believers. This verse highlights the enduring nature of God's love.

Verse 36

- "As it is written, For thy sake we are killed all the day long; we are accounted as sheep for the slaughter."

Commentary: Paul quotes from Psalm 44:22 to emphasize that believers may face persecution and suffering. The quotation reinforces the idea that such hardships are not indicative of God's abandonment but can be part of the Christian experience.

Verse 37

- "Nay, in all these things we are more than conquerors through him that loved us."

Commentary: In contrast to the trials mentioned in verse 35, Paul asserts that believers are "more than conquerors" through Christ's love. Even in the face of adversity, they have victory. This victory is achieved not in their strength but through the love and power of Christ.

Verse 38-39

- "For I am persuaded, that neither death, nor life, nor angels, nor principalities, nor powers, nor things present, nor things to come, nor height, nor depth, nor any other creature, shall be able to separate us from the love of God, which is in Christ Jesus our Lord."

Commentary: Paul concludes this powerful passage with a comprehensive list of potential challenges and entities that cannot separate believers from the love of God. This list is all-encompassing and leaves no room for doubt. Whether in life or in death, believers are secure in God's love, and nothing in all of creation can sever that divine bond. The love of God in Christ is eternally unwavering and unbreakable.

In these verses, Paul reassures believers of the security of their salvation and the unwavering love of God. He emphasizes that no external circumstances, suffering, or opposition can separate them from the love of Christ. This passage serves as a powerful declaration of God's faithfulness and the victorious position of believers in Christ.

CHAPTER 9
God's Sovereign Choice

Romans 9:1-10: God's Sovereign Choice

Verse 1

- "I say the truth in Christ, I lie not, my conscience also bearing me witness in the Holy Ghost,"

Commentary: Paul begins by emphasizing the truth of his words, invoking Christ and the Holy Spirit as witnesses to the sincerity of his statement. This highlights the gravity and significance of the subject he's about to address.

Verse 2

- "That I have great heaviness and continual sorrow in my heart."

Commentary: Paul expresses deep anguish and sorrow in his heart. He is about to address the issue of Israel's rejection of Christ, a topic that deeply grieves him. This verse provides insight into the emotional weight Paul carries as he discusses this matter.

Verse 3

- "For I could wish that myself were accursed from Christ for my brethren, my kinsmen according to the flesh:"

Commentary: Paul's concern for his fellow Jews is so profound that he expresses a willingness to be "accursed from Christ" for their sake. He is willing to endure any suffering or separation from Christ if it meant the salvation of his Jewish kinsmen. This reveals the depth of his love and concern for the salvation of his people.

Verse 4

- "Who are Israelites; to whom pertaineth the adoption, and the glory, and the covenants, and the giving of the law, and the service of God, and the promises;"

Commentary: Paul highlights the unique and privileged position of the Israelites in God's redemptive plan. They were the chosen people, recipients of God's adoption, glory, covenants, the law, service to God, and promises. This is a reminder of God's special relationship with the nation of Israel.

Verse 5

- "Whose are the fathers, and of whom as concerning the flesh Christ came, who is over all, God blessed forever. Amen."

Commentary: Paul underscores the historical lineage and importance of the Israelites, as it was from their ancestors that Christ came in the flesh. He acknowledges the divinity of Christ, describing Him as "God blessed forever," affirming Christ's eternal and divine nature.

Verse 6

- "Not as though the word of God hath taken none effect. For they are not all Israel, which are of Israel:"

Commentary: Here, Paul addresses a critical point. He clarifies that not all who are descended from Israel by blood are truly "Israel." In other words, mere ethnic heritage does not automatically grant a person a place in God's true people. Paul begins to highlight the distinction between physical and spiritual Israel.

Verse 7

- "Neither, because they are the seed of Abraham, are they all children: but, In Isaac shall thy seed be called."

Commentary: Paul uses the example of Abraham's descendants to illustrate his point. Although they are the physical seed of Abraham, not all are considered God's children. Instead, God's promise of blessing and calling was specifically tied to Abraham's son, Isaac, emphasizing that God's choice is not based on lineage alone.

Verse 8

- "That is, They which are the children of the flesh, these are not the children of God: but the children of the promise are counted for the seed."

Commentary: Paul clarifies his argument by distinguishing between "the children of the flesh" and "the children of the promise." He asserts that being a physical descendant of Abraham doesn't automatically make one a child of God. Instead, God's chosen people are those who are children of the promise—those who respond in faith to God's covenant and calling.

Verse 9

- "For this is the word of promise, At this time will I come, and Sarah shall have a son."

Commentary: Paul refers to the promise God made to Abraham and Sarah regarding the birth of their son, Isaac. This promise was a demonstration of God's sovereignty in choosing whom He would bless and call, as Isaac was born in fulfillment of God's word.

Verse 10

- "And not only this; but when Rebecca also had conceived by one, even by our father Isaac;"

Commentary: Paul continues to provide an example, referencing the conception of Jacob and Esau by their parents, Isaac and Rebecca. This example will be further developed in the following verses to illustrate God's sovereign choice and the distinction between physical lineage and spiritual election.

In this passage, Paul introduces the theme of God's sovereign choice in the context of Israel's relationship with God. He emphasizes that being a physical descendant of Israel or Abraham is not enough to secure one's place as God's chosen people. Instead, Paul underscores the significance of faith and God's promise in determining who truly belongs to God's spiritual family. This theme sets the stage for a more extensive discussion of God's sovereign choice in the chapters that follow.

Romans 9:11-20: God's Sovereign Choice and Mercy

Verse 11

- "(For the children being not yet born, neither having done any good or evil, that the purpose of God according to election might stand, not of works, but of him that calleth;)"

Commentary: Paul delves deeper into the theme of God's sovereignty in choosing His people. He points out that God's choice is not based on the children's deeds or actions because they weren't born or had the opportunity to do good or evil. Instead, God's choice is rooted in His divine purpose of election, not human merit or works. It's God's calling that determines their status as His chosen ones.

Verse 12

- "It was said unto her, The elder shall serve the younger."

Commentary: Paul references the prophecy given to Rebekah when she was pregnant with twins, Esau and Jacob. The prophecy indicated that the older, Esau, would serve the younger, Jacob. This declaration demonstrates God's sovereign choice in selecting Jacob, the younger son, as the one through whom His covenant would continue.

Verse 13

- "As it is written, Jacob have I loved, but Esau have I hated."

Commentary: Paul cites Malachi 1:2-3, where God declares His love for Jacob and His hatred for Esau. It's important to understand that this declaration of love and hatred does not imply that God despised Esau personally but rather signifies God's sovereign choice in selecting Jacob as the recipient of His covenant blessings. This demonstrates God's prerogative to choose and call individuals for His purposes.

Verse 14

- "What shall we say then? Is there unrighteousness with God? God forbid."

Commentary: Paul anticipates a potential objection or question from his audience. Some might wonder if God's sovereign choice is unfair or unrighteous. In response, Paul emphatically states, "God forbid" or "certainly not." He rejects any notion of unrighteousness in God's actions and emphasizes His divine authority in making these choices.

Verse 15

- "For he saith to Moses, I will have mercy on whom I will have mercy, and I will have compassion on whom I will have compassion."

Commentary: Paul quotes from Exodus 33:19, where God reveals His sovereign prerogative in showing mercy and compassion. God is not bound by human expectations or standards in His dispensing of mercy. He bestows His mercy and compassion according to His divine will and purpose.

Verse 16

- "So then it is not of him that willeth, nor of him that runneth, but of God that sheweth mercy."

Commentary: Paul underscores that God's mercy is not dependent on human will or effort. It's not something that can be earned or attained through human striving. Instead, God's mercy is entirely a result of His own choice and grace. This reinforces the idea that God's sovereignty is the determining factor in His choice to show mercy.

Verse 17

- "For the scripture saith unto Pharaoh, Even for this same purpose have I raised thee up, that I might show my power in thee, and that my name might be declared throughout all the earth."

Commentary: Paul refers to the example of Pharaoh during the time of the Exodus. God's purpose in raising up Pharaoh was to demonstrate His power and make His name known throughout the earth. This serves as an illustration of God's sovereign authority and His use of individuals and events to achieve His divine purposes.

Verse 18

- "Therefore hath he mercy on whom he will have mercy, and whom he will he hardeneth."

Commentary: Paul reiterates the principle of God's sovereignty in showing mercy and, conversely, in hardening hearts. God's actions are based on His own divine will, and this includes both bestowing mercy and permitting hardness of heart in accordance with His purposes.

Verse 19

- "Thou wilt say then unto me, Why doth he yet find fault? For who hath resisted his will?"

Commentary: Paul anticipates another objection. Some might argue that if God's will is ultimately responsible for everything, how can He find fault with people's actions? The objection is essentially asking how humans can be held responsible if they cannot resist God's will.

Verse 20

- "Nay but, O man, who art thou that repliest against God? Shall the thing formed say to him that formed it, Why hast thou made me thus?"

Commentary: In response to the objection, Paul uses a rhetorical question to emphasize the limited perspective of humanity in questioning God's ways. He points out the audacity of questioning the Creator, likening it to a created being challenging the Creator's design and purpose. This underscores the inherent limitations of human understanding when it comes to comprehending God's sovereignty and wisdom in His choices.

In this passage, Paul delves deeply into the concept of God's sovereign choice, demonstrating that God's decisions are not based on human merit or works. Instead, God's mercy and hardening of hearts are based on His divine purpose and will. The example of Jacob and Esau, as well as God's dealings with Pharaoh, illustrate God's prerogative to show mercy and accomplish His purposes, emphasizing His authority and wisdom. The objections raised and Paul's responses highlight the tension between divine sovereignty and human responsibility, underscoring the limitations of human understanding in fully grasping God's ways.

Romans 9:21-33: God's Sovereignty and Israel's Unbelief

Verse 21

- "Hath not the potter power over the clay, of the same lump to make one vessel unto honour, and another unto dishonour?"

Commentary: Paul uses an analogy of a potter and clay to illustrate God's sovereignty over His creation. Just as a potter has the authority to shape clay into vessels for different purposes, so too does God have the authority to determine the destiny and purpose of individuals. This passage reaffirms the idea that God's choices are not contingent upon human merit but are based on His divine will and purpose.

Verse 22

- "What if God, willing to shew his wrath, and to make his power known, endured with much longsuffering the vessels of wrath fitted to destruction:"

Commentary: Paul explains that God, in demonstrating His wrath and power, has patiently endured those who are "vessels of wrath fitted to destruction." This indicates that even those who ultimately reject God's grace and choose destruction serve a purpose in God's larger plan. His patience allows for the unfolding of His divine purpose, which includes judgment and justice.

Verse 23

- "And that he might make known the riches of his glory on the vessels of mercy, which he had afore prepared unto glory,"

Commentary: In contrast to the vessels of wrath, God's plan also includes "vessels of mercy." These are individuals whom God has "afore prepared unto glory." The purpose of these vessels of mercy is to make known the riches of God's glory. In God's divine plan, both mercy and justice serve to reveal His attributes and purposes.

Verse 24

- "Even us, whom he hath called, not of the Jews only, but also of the Gentiles?"

Commentary: Paul underscores that God's call extends to both Jews and Gentiles. The inclusion of Gentiles in God's plan is a significant theme in Romans, emphasizing that God's purpose transcends national or ethnic boundaries.

Verse 25

- "As he saith also in Osee, I will call them my people, which were not my people; and her beloved, which was not beloved."

Commentary: Paul quotes from the prophet Hosea (Hosea 2:23) to illustrate the inclusion of those who were previously not considered part of God's people. This verse serves as a reminder of God's ability to call and transform those who were once outsiders into His beloved people.

Verse 26

- "And it shall come to pass, that in the place where it was said unto them, Ye are not my people; there shall they be called the children of the living God."

Commentary: Paul continues to quote from Hosea (Hosea 1:10), highlighting the divine transformation that turns those who were once told "Ye are not my people" into "the children of the living God." This emphasizes God's capacity to redefine and call people to be part of His family.

Verse 27

- "Esaias also crieth concerning Israel, Though the number of the children of Israel be as the sand of the sea, a remnant shall be saved:"

Commentary: Paul quotes from the prophet Isaiah (Isaiah 10:22) to emphasize that, despite the large number of Israel's descendants, only a remnant will be saved. This serves as a reminder that the fulfillment of God's promises is not based on sheer numbers but on faith and His sovereign choice.

Verse 28

- "For he will finish the work, and cut it short in righteousness: because a short work will the Lord make upon the earth."

Commentary: This verse suggests that God's work of salvation will be brought to a conclusion swiftly and righteously. His purpose will be accomplished in a manner that reflects His justice and wisdom.

Verse 29

- "And as Esaias said before, Except the Lord of Sabaoth had left us a seed, we had been as Sodoma, and been made like unto Gomorrha."

Commentary: Paul refers to the prophecy of Isaiah (Isaiah 1:9) to highlight the idea that only a remnant, a "seed," is preserved by the Lord's intervention. Without this divine intervention, the fate of Israel would have resembled that of Sodom and Gomorrah—total destruction.

Verse 30

- "What shall we say then? That the Gentiles, which followed not after righteousness, have attained to righteousness, even the righteousness which is of faith."

Commentary: Paul addresses the contrast between Jews and Gentiles in attaining righteousness. He notes that the Gentiles, who were not actively pursuing righteousness through the law, have attained righteousness through faith in Christ. This underscores the theme of God's inclusive plan, extending salvation to those outside the Jewish covenant.

Verse 31

Romans 9:31-33: The Pursuit of Righteousness by Faith

Verse 31

- "But Israel, which followed after the law of righteousness, hath not attained to the law of righteousness."

Commentary: Paul continues to contrast the response of Israel and the Gentiles to the pursuit of righteousness. Israel, being recipients of the Mosaic Law and pursuing righteousness through adherence to it, did not fully attain the goal of righteousness. This highlights the limitations of law-based righteousness, as it cannot justify or save a person. Instead, it reveals one's inability to fulfill the law's requirements perfectly.

Verse 32

- "Wherefore? Because they sought it not by faith, but as it were by the works of the law. For they stumbled at that stumbling stone;"

Commentary: Paul explains why Israel fell short in their pursuit of righteousness. It was because they sought righteousness through the works of the law rather than by faith. Their focus on legalistic observance hindered them from recognizing the true source of righteousness, which is faith in Christ. Furthermore, Paul introduces the concept of a "stumbling stone," which represents an obstacle or stumbling block. In this context, it refers to Christ as the stumbling block for those who sought righteousness through works rather than faith.

Verse 33

- "As it is written, Behold, I lay in Sion a stumbling stone and rock of offence: and whosoever believeth on him shall not be ashamed."

Commentary: Paul cites two Old Testament passages to support his point. The first part, "Behold, I lay in Sion a stumbling stone and rock of offence," is from Isaiah 8:14 and Psalm 118:22. It underscores that Christ, while the cornerstone of faith for believers, becomes a stumbling block for those who reject Him.

The second part, "and whosoever believeth on him shall not be ashamed," is a promise from Isaiah 28:16. It assures that anyone who places their faith in Christ will not be disappointed or put to shame. Faith in Christ as the means of righteousness is the path to salvation.

In these verses, Paul continues to emphasize the crucial distinction between seeking righteousness through the works of the law and attaining it by faith in Christ. Israel's failure to attain righteousness was due to their reliance on legalistic observance rather than faith. Christ is presented as the cornerstone for believers but a stumbling block for those who seek righteousness through their own efforts. The message is clear: salvation comes through faith in Christ, not through human works or the law. Those who believe in Him will find their faith rewarded, and they will not be put to shame.

CHAPTER 10
The Righteous of Faith

Romans 10:1-10: The Righteousness of Faith

Verse 1

- "Brethren, my heart's desire and prayer to God for Israel is, that they might be saved."

Commentary: Paul expresses his deep concern and heartfelt desire for the salvation of his fellow Israelites. He is earnestly praying to God for their redemption, highlighting his deep love and care for his own people.

Verse 2

- "For I bear them record that they have a zeal of God, but not according to knowledge."

Commentary: Paul acknowledges that the Israelites have a zeal for God, but he points out that their zeal is not accompanied by accurate knowledge. In other words, they have a fervent religious commitment, but it lacks a full understanding of God's righteousness, grace, and the means of salvation.

Verse 3

- "For they being ignorant of God's righteousness, and going about to establish their own righteousness, have not submitted themselves unto the righteousness of God."

Commentary: This verse highlights the core issue: the Israelites are ignorant of God's righteousness. Instead of accepting God's righteousness by faith, they attempt to establish their own righteousness through works of the law. They have not humbly submitted themselves to God's righteousness offered through faith in Christ.

Verse 4

- "For Christ is the end of the law for righteousness to everyone that believeth."

Commentary: Paul declares a fundamental truth: Christ is the culmination or fulfillment of the law with regard to righteousness. In other words, the purpose and fulfillment of the law's demands are found in Christ, and this is accessible to anyone who believes in Him. Faith in Christ is the key to righteousness, not striving to fulfill the law on one's own.

Verse 5

- "For Moses describeth the righteousness which is of the law, That the man which doeth those things shall live by them."

Commentary: Paul refers to a principle from the law as described by Moses (Leviticus 18:5). According to the law, one could obtain righteousness by perfectly obeying its commands. However, the problem is that no one can fully comply with the law's demands. Therefore, this path to righteousness proves impossible for fallen humanity.

Verse 6

- "But the righteousness which is of faith speaketh on this wise, Say not in thine heart, Who shall ascend into heaven? (that is, to bring Christ down from above:)"

Commentary: Paul contrasts the righteousness that comes through faith with the righteousness based on the law. The righteousness of faith does not require extraordinary efforts like ascending into heaven to bring Christ down. It's not a matter of human achievement but a matter of faith in Christ's finished work.

Verse 7

- "Or, Who shall descend into the deep? (that is, to bring up Christ again from the dead.)"

Commentary: Similarly, faith in Christ's righteousness doesn't involve descending into the deep, symbolizing a futile effort to bring Christ back from the dead. Christ's resurrection is God's act, and faith simply receives the benefits of this redemptive work.

Verse 8

- "But what saith it? The word is nigh thee, even in thy mouth, and in thy heart: that is, the word of faith, which we preach;"

Commentary: Paul emphasizes the accessibility of the word of faith. This word is near, available, and easily received—it's in one's mouth and heart. This underscores the simplicity of the gospel message, which is based on faith in Christ, not on complex human efforts.

Verse 9

- "That if thou shalt confess with thy mouth the Lord Jesus, and shalt believe in thine heart that God hath raised him from the dead, thou shalt be saved."

Commentary: This verse articulates the essence of salvation through faith. It involves two essential components: confessing with one's mouth that Jesus is Lord and believing in one's heart that God raised Him from the dead. Salvation is granted to those who genuinely believe in the resurrection of Christ and confess Him as Lord.

Verse 10

- "For with the heart man believeth unto righteousness; and with the mouth confession is made unto salvation."

Commentary: This verse elucidates the relationship between faith and salvation. Righteousness is obtained by believing in one's heart, and salvation is realized through confessing with one's mouth. Both faith and confession play integral roles in the process of salvation.

In these verses, Paul underscores the importance of faith in Christ as the means of attaining righteousness and salvation. He contrasts the futile efforts to establish one's righteousness through the law with the simplicity of faith in Christ. The core message is that faith and confession of Christ as Lord are the keys to salvation, accessible to all who believe.

Romans 10:11-21: The Gospel's Widespread Offer and Israel's Response

Verse 11

- "For the scripture saith, Whosoever believeth on him shall not be ashamed."

Commentary: Paul quotes from Isaiah 28:16 to reinforce the idea that faith in Christ leads to salvation without shame. This verse highlights the universal aspect of the gospel: it is available to "whosoever," without distinction.

Verse 12

- "For there is no difference between the Jew and the Greek: for the same Lord over all is rich unto all that call upon him."

Commentary: In this verse, Paul emphasizes the universality of the gospel's offer. There is no distinction between Jews and Gentiles; the same Lord is generous to all who call upon Him in faith. This underscores the inclusivity of God's salvation plan.

Verse 13

- "For whosoever shall call upon the name of the Lord shall be saved."

Commentary: Paul reiterates the universality of salvation: anyone who calls upon the name of the Lord, regardless of their background, shall be saved. This verse emphasizes the simplicity of salvation through a sincere and heartfelt confession of faith in Christ.

Verse 14

- "How then shall they call on him in whom they have not believed? and how shall they believe in him of whom they have not heard? and how shall they hear without a preacher?"

Commentary: Paul delves into the process of salvation, highlighting the necessity of preaching and hearing the gospel. People must first hear the message of Christ in order to believe in Him and call upon His name for salvation. This underscores the role of preachers and evangelists in sharing the good news.

Verse 15

- "And how shall they preach, except they be sent? as it is written, How beautiful are the feet of them that preach the gospel of peace, and bring glad tidings of good things!"

Commentary: Paul emphasizes the role of sending and commissioning messengers to preach the gospel. He quotes from Isaiah 52:7 to emphasize the beauty of those who bring the good news of peace and glad tidings. This verse reinforces the importance of the mission of spreading the gospel to the unreached.

Verse 16

- "But they have not all obeyed the gospel. For Esaias saith, Lord, who hath believed our report?"

Commentary: Paul acknowledges that not everyone who hears the gospel responds in faith. He quotes from Isaiah 53:1, where the prophet expresses wonder about who would believe their report. This underscores the challenge of human response to the gospel, even when it is preached.

Verse 17

- "So then faith cometh by hearing, and hearing by the word of God."

Commentary: Paul reaffirms the vital connection between faith and hearing the word of God. Faith is awakened and nourished through the hearing of God's word. This reinforces the importance of Scripture and preaching in the process of salvation.

Verse 18

- "But I say, Have they not heard? Yes verily, their sound went into all the earth, and their words unto the ends of the world."

Commentary: Paul alludes to Psalm 19:4, emphasizing that the message of the gospel has been proclaimed to the ends of the earth. This underscores the global reach of the gospel and the responsibility of all nations to hear and respond to it.

Verse 19

- "But I say, Did not Israel know? First Moses saith, I will provoke you to jealousy by them that are no people, and by a foolish nation I will anger you."

Commentary: Paul quotes from Deuteronomy 32:21 to show that God had prophesied about provoking Israel to jealousy by extending His blessings and calling to those outside the nation—Gentiles. This serves as a reminder of Israel's unbelief and the inclusion of Gentiles in God's plan.

Verse 20

- "But Esaias is very bold, and saith, I was found of them that sought me not; I was made manifest unto them that asked not after me."

Commentary: Paul quotes from Isaiah 65:1, emphasizing that God revealed Himself to people who were not actively seeking Him or asking after Him. This highlights the graciousness of God in reaching out to the Gentiles who were not part of the Jewish covenant.

Verse 21

- "But to Israel he saith, All day long I have stretched forth my hands unto a disobedient and gainsaying people."

Commentary: In a concluding note, Paul references Isaiah 65:2 to express God's extended offer of grace and outreach to Israel. However, this verse also reveals Israel's stubbornness and disobedience in rejecting God's call, which plays a prominent role in the larger context of Romans.

In these verses, Paul emphasizes the universal offer of salvation to both Jews and Gentiles, stressing the necessity of hearing the gospel and responding in faith. He underscores the role of preachers and the spread of the gospel to the ends of the earth. Despite the global reach of the message, he points out that not all will believe, and he alludes to Israel's unbelief as part of God's plan to extend His blessings to Gentiles.

CHAPTER 11
The Remnant of Israel

Romans 11:1-10: The Remnant of Israel

Verse 1

- "I say then, Hath God cast away his people? God forbid. For I also am an Israelite, of the seed of Abraham, of the tribe of Benjamin."

Commentary: Paul begins this section by addressing a question: Has God rejected His people, Israel? His emphatic response is "God forbid." He passionately denies the idea that God has completely abandoned His chosen people. To support his point, he notes that he himself is an Israelite from the tribe of Benjamin, underscoring that God's covenant with Israel remains significant.

Verse 2

- "God hath not cast away his people which he foreknew. Wot ye not what the scripture saith of Elias? how he maketh intercession to God against Israel, saying,"

Commentary: Paul reinforces his point that God has not rejected His people by referring to the example of the prophet Elijah (Elias). He reminds the readers that even Elijah, in his time, interceded to God on behalf of Israel despite their waywardness. This historical illustration highlights God's enduring relationship with His people.

Verse 3

- "Lord, they have killed thy prophets, and digged down thine altars; and I am left alone, and they seek my life."

Commentary: Paul quotes Elijah's complaint to God from 1 Kings 19:10. This lament highlights Israel's rebellion, as they had killed God's prophets and destroyed His altars. Elijah's feeling of being the only faithful one emphasizes the spiritual decline of Israel at that time.

Verse 4

- "But what saith the answer of God unto him? I have reserved to myself seven thousand men, who have not bowed the knee to the image of Baal."

Commentary: Paul immediately follows Elijah's complaint with God's response to him from 1 Kings 19:18. God reassured Elijah that there were still seven thousand faithful individuals in Israel who had not succumbed to idolatry. This passage demonstrates God's preservation of a remnant of faithful people within Israel, even during difficult times.

Verse 5

- "Even so then at this present time also there is a remnant according to the election of grace."

Commentary: Paul draws a parallel between the situation in Elijah's time and the present. Just as there was a remnant in Elijah's day, there is also a remnant of faithful Israelites at the time when he was writing. This remnant exists not due to their merit but as a result of God's gracious election.

Verse 6

- "And if by grace, then is it no more of works: otherwise grace is no more grace. But if it be of works, then is it no more grace: otherwise work is no more work."

Commentary: Paul emphasizes the clear distinction between grace and works. If salvation were based on works, it would no longer be by grace. Conversely, if it were based on grace, it cannot be earned through works. This underscores the principle that salvation is entirely a result of God's unmerited favor, not human achievement.

Verse 7

- "What then? Israel hath not obtained that which he seeketh for; but the election hath obtained it, and the rest were blinded."

Commentary: Paul acknowledges that as a whole, Israel had not fully obtained what they sought, which was righteousness and salvation. However, the elect, or the remnant chosen by God, did obtain it. The rest, the majority, were blinded or hardened to the message of salvation due to their unbelief.

Verse 8

- "(According as it is written, God hath given them the spirit of slumber, eyes that they should not see, and ears that they should not hear;) unto this day."

Commentary: Paul quotes from Isaiah 29:10 to explain Israel's spiritual condition. This condition involves a "spirit of slumber," symbolizing spiritual insensitivity, where their eyes do not perceive the truth and their ears do not hear the message of salvation. This spiritual state persisted until Paul's time.

Verse 9

- "And David saith, Let their table be made a snare, and a trap, and a stumbling block, and a recompence unto them:"

Commentary: Paul quotes from Psalm 69:22-23 to further illustrate the consequences of Israel's unbelief. David's words in the psalm indicate that what should have been a source of sustenance and blessing became a snare, a trap, and a stumbling block for those who rejected God's message. This serves as a warning of the perils of unbelief.

Verse 10

- "Let their eyes be darkened, that they may not see, and bow down their back always."

Commentary: Paul concludes this section by quoting from Psalm 69:23. The darkening of their eyes signifies continued spiritual blindness, and the imagery of bowed backs suggests the weight of their unbelief and the consequences it brings.

In these verses, Paul addresses the question of whether God has completely rejected Israel. He emphasizes the existence of a faithful remnant within Israel, highlighting that salvation is based on God's gracious election rather than human works. He cites historical examples, such as Elijah and David, to illustrate God's preservation of a remnant and the consequences of unbelief. The central theme remains God's sovereignty and His ongoing plan for Israel, which extends beyond their present unbelief.

Romans 11:11-20: The Salvation of the Gentiles and Israel's Future

Verse 11

- "I say then, Have they stumbled that they should fall? God forbid: but rather through their fall salvation is come unto the Gentiles, for to provoke them to jealousy."

Commentary: Paul addresses the question of whether Israel's stumbling resulted in their permanent fall from grace. His response is a firm "God forbid." While some Israelites rejected Christ, it did not mean the complete rejection of the nation. Instead, their fall led to a significant outcome: salvation was extended to the Gentiles. This served a dual purpose: the salvation of the Gentiles and provoking Israel to jealousy, which might ultimately lead to their salvation.

Verse 12

- "Now if the fall of them be the riches of the world, and the diminishing of them the riches of the Gentiles; how much more their fulness?"

Commentary: Paul highlights the positive consequences of Israel's fall. Their fall opened the door to the riches of salvation for the Gentiles. This leads to the question of how much greater will the outcome be when Israel, as a whole, turns to God in faith. The expectation is that Israel's eventual full acceptance of Christ will bring about even greater blessings.

Verse 13

- "For I speak to you Gentiles, inasmuch as I am the apostle of the Gentiles, I magnify mine office:"

Commentary: Paul addresses his primarily Gentile audience in Rome and underscores his role as the apostle to the Gentiles. He magnifies or honors his apostolic calling, which includes delivering the message of Christ to the Gentiles and facilitating their inclusion in God's plan.

Verse 14

- "If by any means I may provoke to emulation them which are my flesh, and might save some of them."

Commentary: Paul expresses his desire to provoke a sense of emulation or jealousy among his fellow Israelites, who share his Jewish heritage. He hopes that through the salvation of the Gentiles, some of his fellow Israelites may be moved to embrace faith in Christ and be saved.

Verse 15

- "For if the casting away of them be the reconciling of the world, what shall the receiving of them be, but life from the dead?"

Commentary: Paul once again reflects on the positive outcomes of Israel's temporary rejection. Their rejection led to the reconciling of the world through the gospel's outreach to the Gentiles. If this was the result of their fall, then their eventual receiving or acceptance will bring about an even more significant spiritual revival—a metaphorical "life from the dead."

Verse 16

- "For if the firstfruit be holy, the lump is also holy: and if the root be holy, so are the branches."

Commentary: Paul uses an agricultural analogy to explain the relationship between Israel and the Gentiles. The "firstfruit" and the "root" represent the patriarchs and the foundation of Israel. If they are considered holy, it implies that the whole nation, represented as the "lump" and the "branches," has a sanctified status. This highlights the unique spiritual heritage of Israel.

Verse 17

- "And if some of the branches be broken off, and thou, being a wild olive tree, wert graffed in among them, and with them partakest of the root and fatness of the olive tree;"

Commentary: In continuation of the agricultural metaphor, Paul explains that some of the natural branches (Israelites) were broken off due to unbelief. The wild olive tree represents the Gentiles, who were grafted in among the natural branches. This grafting allows them to share in the spiritual heritage and blessings of the original olive tree (Israel).

Verse 18

- "Boast not against the branches. But if thou boast, thou bearest not the root, but the root thee."

Commentary: Paul cautions the Gentiles not to boast or feel superior to the natural branches (Israelites) that were broken off due to unbelief. He reminds them that they are dependent on the root (the patriarchs and God's promises to Israel) for their spiritual nourishment and blessings. It's not a reason for pride but humility.

Verse 19

- "Thou wilt say then, The branches were broken off, that I might be graffed in."

Commentary: Paul anticipates a possible objection from the Gentiles, who might think that the natural branches were broken off to make room for their grafting. He acknowledges this, but he will provide a caution in the following verse.

Verse 20

- "Well; because of unbelief they were broken off, and thou standest by faith. Be not highminded, but fear:"

Commentary: Paul clarifies that the natural branches were indeed broken off due to unbelief, not to elevate the Gentiles. He advises the Gentiles not to become prideful but to maintain a humble and reverential attitude, rooted in faith. This serves as a reminder that faith is the basis of their inclusion, not their own merit.

In these verses, Paul discusses the relationship between the salvation of the Gentiles and the future of Israel. He emphasizes the positive outcomes of Israel's temporary fall, including the salvation of the Gentiles and the eventual restoration of Israel. The passages employ metaphors to illustrate these concepts, highlighting the interconnection between Gentile believers and the Jewish heritage. Paul also warns against pride and encourages humility in light of God's plan for both Jews and Gentiles.

Romans 11:21-30: The Mercy and Call of God

Verse 21

- "For if God spared not the natural branches, take heed lest he also spare not thee."

Commentary: Paul issues a stern warning to the Gentile believers. He references the "natural branches," which represent the Israelites. If God did not spare them due to their unbelief, Gentile believers should take heed and not become complacent. This warning reminds them of the importance of continuing in faith and not taking their position for granted.

Verse 22

- "Behold therefore the goodness and severity of God: on them which fell, severity; but toward thee, goodness, if thou continue in his goodness: otherwise thou also shalt be cut off."

Commentary: Paul contrasts the aspects of God's character—His goodness and severity. The Israelites experienced God's severity due to their unbelief. In contrast, the Gentile believers have experienced His goodness through faith. However, this goodness is conditional on their continued faith. If they do not persist in faith, they, too, could face separation from God's blessings.

Verse 23

- "And they also, if they abide not still in unbelief, shall be graffed in: for God is able to graff them in again."

Commentary: Paul offers hope for the Israelites who were broken off due to unbelief. If they turn from unbelief and embrace faith, God can graft them back into His covenant blessings. This underscores God's mercy and His ability to restore those who repent and believe.

Verse 24

- "For if thou wert cut out of the olive tree which is wild by nature, and wert graffed contrary to nature into a good olive tree: how much more shall these, which be the natural branches, be graffed into their own olive tree?"

Commentary: Paul reiterates the idea of grafting, illustrating how the Gentiles, being like wild olive branches, were grafted into the good olive tree, representing God's covenant with Israel. He emphasizes that it would be even more natural and likely for the Israelites, as the "natural branches," to be regrafted into their own olive tree—their original covenant relationship with God.

Verse 25

- "For I would not, brethren, that ye should be ignorant of this mystery, lest ye should be wise in your own conceits; that blindness in part is happened to Israel, until the fulness of the Gentiles be come in."

Commentary: Paul introduces a mysterious aspect of God's plan. He does not want the Gentile believers to be ignorant of this truth. He asserts that a partial blindness has come upon Israel for a specific period—until the full number of Gentiles has come to faith. This implies a divine timetable for the salvation of both Jews and Gentiles.

Verse 26

- "And so all Israel shall be saved: as it is written, There shall come out of Sion the Deliverer, and shall turn away ungodliness from Jacob:"

Commentary: Paul predicts a future event when "all Israel" will experience salvation. He quotes from Isaiah 59:20, which speaks of a Deliverer coming from Zion (a reference to Christ) who will remove ungodliness from Jacob (a reference to Israel). This affirms God's enduring commitment to redeem and restore His people.

Verse 27

- "For this is my covenant unto them, when I shall take away their sins."

Commentary: Paul emphasizes that the future salvation of Israel is in keeping with God's covenant promises. He echoes the prophetic promise of the removal of sins, indicating a national forgiveness and reconciliation with God.

Verse 28

- "As concerning the gospel, they are enemies for your sakes: but as touching the election, they are beloved for the fathers' sakes."

Commentary: Paul acknowledges that, concerning the gospel, the Israelites may be perceived as enemies due to their unbelief. However, in the context of God's election and His covenant with the patriarchs (Abraham, Isaac, and Jacob), they are still beloved by God.

Verse 29

- "For the gifts and calling of God are without repentance."

Commentary: Paul underscores the unchanging nature of God's gifts and calling. Once God has made a promise or granted a gift, He does not change His mind. His covenant with Israel, including His promises of blessing and salvation, remains steadfast.

Verse 30

- "For as ye in times past have not believed God, yet have now obtained mercy through their unbelief:"

Commentary: Paul reminds the Gentile believers that they, too, were once in a state of unbelief. However, they have now received God's mercy, partly as a result of the unbelief of the Israelites. This highlights the interconnectedness of God's plan for both Jews and Gentiles.

In these verses, Paul addresses the relationship between the Gentile believers and the future of Israel. He underscores the need for continued faith among the Gentiles and the possibility of the Israelites being regrafted into God's covenant. He also introduces the mystery of a future salvation for all Israel and emphasizes God's unchanging promises and calling. Paul's message is one of hope and the enduring mercy of God for all who believe.

Romans 11:31-35: The Depths of God's Wisdom and Knowledge

Verse 31

- "Even so have these also now not believed, that through your mercy they also may obtain mercy."

Commentary: Paul continues to discuss the relationship between Gentile believers and Israel. He notes that, just as the Israelites had been disobedient, so too the Gentiles, who have now received God's mercy. The purpose of this mercy to the Gentiles is to provoke the Israelites to faith so that they, too, may receive God's mercy. It reflects God's overarching plan for the salvation of all.

Verse 32

- "For God hath concluded them all in unbelief, that he might have mercy upon all."

Commentary: This verse emphasizes God's divine plan. He has allowed both Jews and Gentiles to experience unbelief, not to condemn them but rather to extend His mercy to all. It is a demonstration of God's inclusive and redemptive purpose to offer salvation to both groups.

Verse 33

- "O the depth of the riches both of the wisdom and knowledge of God! how unsearchable are his judgments, and his ways past finding out!"

Commentary: Paul, moved by the depth of God's plan for salvation, erupts in praise. He marvels at the vastness of God's wisdom and knowledge, which surpass human comprehension. God's judgments and ways are unsearchable and beyond human understanding, highlighting the profound and mysterious nature of His divine plan.

Verse 34

- "For who hath known the mind of the Lord? or who hath been his counsellor?"

Commentary: Paul emphasizes the impossibility of anyone fully comprehending the mind of the Lord or acting as His counselor. God's ways and decisions are beyond human capacity for insight, advice, or manipulation. This statement underscores the divine sovereignty of God.

Verse 35

- "Or who hath first given to him, and it shall be recompensed unto him again?"

Commentary: Paul asks a rhetorical question to highlight that no one can claim to have given something to God first, expecting to be repaid by Him. In other words, no one can demand that God owes them something. It underscores the idea that all is ultimately from God, and humans can never merit or manipulate His mercy.

These verses in Romans 11 emphasize the profound depth of God's wisdom and knowledge in His plan for the salvation of both Jews and Gentiles. The mystery of His mercy, the unsearchable nature of His judgments, and His sovereignty are all themes that reflect the richness of God's plan. These verses invite awe and reverence for the Creator's profound and inscrutable ways.

CHAPTER 12
Living Sacrifices and Genuine Love

Romans 12:1-10: Living Sacrifices and Genuine Love

Verse 1

- "I beseech you therefore, brethren, by the mercies of God, that ye present your bodies a living sacrifice, holy, acceptable unto God, which is your reasonable service."

Commentary: Paul opens this chapter with a plea to the believers in Rome. He urges them to offer their entire lives as living sacrifices to God. This is an act of consecration, dedicating themselves wholly to God's service. The phrase "living sacrifice" is significant, as it conveys the idea of a continuous commitment, marked by holiness and acceptability. Paul emphasizes that this act of dedication is a reasonable and logical response to God's abundant mercies and grace.

Verse 2

- "And be not conformed to this world: but be ye transformed by the renewing of your mind, that ye may prove what is that good, and acceptable, and perfect, will of God."

Commentary: Paul encourages believers not to conform to the patterns and values of the world. Instead, they should undergo a transformation by renewing their minds. This renewal involves a change in perspective, priorities, and values. The purpose of this transformation is to discern and experience God's good, acceptable, and perfect will. It reflects the idea that a renewed mind aligns more closely with God's purpose and plan.

Verse 3

- "For I say, through the grace given unto me, to every man that is among you, not to think of himself more highly than he ought to think; but to think soberly, according as God hath dealt to every man the measure of faith."

Commentary: Paul humbly asserts his apostolic authority, granted by God's grace. He advises believers not to have an inflated view of themselves but to think with sober judgment. This humility and self-awareness are important in the Christian community, where each individual is called to serve according to the measure of faith granted by God. It promotes a balanced and harmonious function within the body of believers.

Verse 4

- "For as we have many members in one body, and all members have not the same office:"

Commentary: Paul employs the metaphor of the human body to illustrate the diversity of spiritual gifts and roles within the Christian community. Just as the body has various parts with distinct functions, so too does the church. Each believer has a unique role to play, and no one gift or office is identical.

Verse 5

- "So we, being many, are one body in Christ, and every one members one of another."

Commentary: Paul emphasizes the unity of believers in Christ. Despite their diversity in gifts and roles, they are one body. This interconnectedness signifies the sense of community and mutual dependence that characterizes the church. It's a reminder of the importance of working together in harmony.

Verse 6

- "Having then gifts differing according to the grace that is given to us, whether prophecy, let us prophesy according to the proportion of faith;"

Commentary: Paul acknowledges the diversity of spiritual gifts bestowed on believers, with each gift being a result of God's grace. He mentions prophecy as an example and encourages those with this gift to prophesy according to their level of faith. This emphasizes that the exercise of spiritual gifts should align with one's measure of faith and be guided by God's grace.

Verse 7

- "Or ministry, let us wait on our ministering: or he that teacheth, on teaching;"

Commentary: Paul continues to enumerate various spiritual gifts and the manner in which they should be used. Those with the gift of serving (ministry) should serve diligently. Those gifted in teaching should focus on teaching effectively. These exhortations highlight the importance of faithfully using one's gifts in service to the Christian community.

Verse 8

- "Or he that exhorteth, on exhortation: he that giveth, let him do it with simplicity; he that ruleth, with diligence; he that sheweth mercy, with cheerfulness."

Commentary: Paul lists more spiritual gifts, emphasizing how each should be exercised. Exhorters should be dedicated to encouraging others. Those who give should do so with sincerity and without ulterior motives. Leaders should govern with diligence and responsibility. Those who show mercy should do so with a joyful and compassionate spirit.

Verse 9

- "Let love be without dissimulation. Abhor that which is evil; cleave to that which is good."

Commentary: Paul underscores the centrality of genuine love in the Christian life. Love should be sincere, without hypocrisy. It should be characterized by a strong aversion to evil and a firm commitment to what is good. This verse encapsulates the essence of Christian love in action.

Verse 10

- "Be kindly affectioned one to another with brotherly love; in honour preferring one another;"

Commentary: Paul encourages believers to have warm, brotherly affection for one another, demonstrating love and care within the Christian community. Additionally, he emphasizes the principle of preferring one another in honor, highlighting a spirit of humility and mutual respect. This verse speaks to the importance of fostering a loving and harmonious Christian fellowship.

In these verses, Paul instructs believers to live as living sacrifices, offering their whole lives to God. He emphasizes the need for transformed thinking, humility, and the exercise of spiritual gifts within the Christian community. Love, both sincere and brotherly, is central to Christian living, fostering unity and mutual respect. These verses provide practical guidance on how to live out the Christian faith in the context of a loving and diverse community of believers.

Romans 12:11-21: Christian Conduct and Love in Action

Verse 11

- "Not slothful in business; fervent in spirit; serving the Lord;"

Commentary: Paul instructs believers to be diligent in their worldly affairs and responsibilities. They are to be enthusiastic and passionate in their spirits, maintaining their fervor in serving the Lord. This verse encourages a strong work ethic in both secular and spiritual matters.

Verse 12

- "Rejoicing in hope; patient in tribulation; continuing instant in prayer;"

Commentary: Paul highlights the Christian's attitude in various life situations. Believers are to maintain joy and hope in the anticipation of God's promises. They should demonstrate patience and endurance during times of tribulation and difficulty. A commitment to persistent prayer, staying in communication with God, is essential in navigating life's challenges.

Verse 13

- "Distributing to the necessity of saints; given to hospitality."

Commentary: Paul calls believers to be generous and compassionate. They are to share with fellow believers who are in need, contributing to the welfare of the saints. Additionally, practicing hospitality is encouraged, demonstrating a welcoming and caring attitude toward others.

Verse 14

- "Bless them which persecute you: bless, and curse not."

Commentary: In the face of persecution or mistreatment, Paul advises believers to respond with blessings instead of cursing. This reflects the Christian principle of responding to hostility with love and goodwill. It is a powerful testament to the transforming work of Christ in one's life.

Verse 15

- "Rejoice with them that do rejoice, and weep with them that weep."

Commentary: This verse underscores the importance of empathy within the Christian community. Believers are to share in the joys and sorrows of fellow believers, rejoicing in their triumphs and offering comfort and support in times of sadness. It highlights the concept of Christian fellowship and mutual care.

Verse 16

- "Be of the same mind one toward another. Mind not high things, but condescend to men of low estate. Be not wise in your own conceits."

Commentary: Paul encourages unity and humility among believers. They are to have a harmonious attitude towards one another, avoiding arrogance or pride. Rather, they should cultivate a spirit of lowliness, relating to individuals of varying social and economic backgrounds with respect. This promotes a spirit of genuine Christian community.

Verse 17

- "Recompense to no man evil for evil. Provide things honest in the sight of all men."

Commentary: Paul teaches believers to refrain from seeking revenge or returning evil for evil. Instead, they should maintain a reputation for honesty and integrity in their interactions with all people. This reflects the ethical character expected of Christians.

Verse 18

- "If it be possible, as much as lieth in you, live peaceably with all men."

Commentary: Paul acknowledges that it may not always be possible to live in peace with everyone due to external factors beyond one's control. Nevertheless, he encourages believers to do everything within their power to pursue peace and harmony in their relationships with others. This promotes the Christian ideal of seeking reconciliation and unity whenever possible.

Verse 19

- "Dearly beloved, avenge not yourselves, but rather give place unto wrath: for it is written, Vengeance is mine; I will repay, saith the Lord."

Commentary: Paul strongly advises against personal vengeance. Believers are to yield to God's justice and timing, recognizing that it is God's prerogative to bring about justice and retribution. The quote, "Vengeance is mine; I will repay," reinforces God's role as the ultimate Judge and Avenger.

Verse 20

- "Therefore, if thine enemy hunger, feed him; if he thirst, give him drink: for in so doing thou shalt heap coals of fire on his head."

Commentary: Paul challenges believers to respond to their enemies with kindness and compassion. By meeting the needs of their adversaries, they may elicit a sense of guilt or conviction, symbolized by "heaping coals of fire on his head." This approach is rooted in the principle of overcoming evil with good, aiming to bring about reconciliation and transformation in one's enemies.

Verse 21

- "Be not overcome of evil, but overcome evil with good."

Commentary: Paul concludes this section with a powerful admonition. Believers are urged not to allow evil to conquer them, but rather to conquer evil through acts of goodness and love. This encapsulates the Christian principle of responding to hatred and malevolence with love and benevolence, ultimately demonstrating the transformative power of God's love.

In these verses, Paul provides practical guidance for Christian living and conduct. He emphasizes the importance of diligence, empathy, humility, forgiveness, and love in the life of a believer. These principles promote harmonious relationships within the Christian community and serve as a testimony to the transformative power of God's grace and love.

CHAPTER 13

Submission to Authority and Love

Romans 13:1-14: Submission to Authority and Love

Verse 1

- "Let every soul be subject unto the higher powers. For there is no power but of God: the powers that be are ordained of God."

Commentary: Paul begins this chapter by addressing the concept of submission to governing authorities. He asserts that every person should be subject to the governing authorities established by God. This reflects the principle of recognizing the divine origin of earthly authorities, and it calls for obedience to established laws and institutions.

Verse 2

- "Whosoever, therefore, resisteth the power, resisteth the ordinance of God: and they that resist shall receive to themselves damnation."

Commentary: Paul underscores the gravity of resisting the governing authorities. Those who resist not only oppose the human order but also resist God's ordained structure. Such resistance carries consequences, as it can lead to judgment or punishment. This reinforces the importance of lawful and orderly conduct within society.

Verse 3

- "For rulers are not a terror to good works, but to the evil. Wilt thou then not be afraid of the power? do that which is good, and thou shalt have praise of the same:"

Commentary: Paul clarifies the role of rulers or authorities. Their function is to restrain and penalize evil deeds, not to be a threat to those who do good. He encourages obedience to the law as a means to avoid fear of authority. When individuals do what is good and just, they are likely to receive commendation and approval from the governing authorities.

Verse 4

- "For he is the minister of God to thee for good. But if thou do that which is evil, be afraid; for he beareth not the sword in vain: for he is the minister of God, a revenger to execute wrath upon him that doeth evil."

Commentary: Paul further explains the role of authorities as ministers of God for the well-being of society. They serve as instruments of God's justice and protection. When individuals engage in evil actions, they should be apprehensive because authorities are authorized to wield the sword, signifying their capacity to enforce consequences upon wrongdoers.

Verse 5

- "Wherefore ye must needs be subject, not only for wrath but also for conscience' sake."

Commentary: Paul provides the motivation for submission to authorities. Believers should submit not only to avoid punishment (wrath) but also for the sake of conscience. This implies that obedience to earthly authorities aligns with one's Christian conscience, reflecting a commitment to lawful and ethical behavior.

Verse 6

- "For this cause pay ye tribute also: for they are God's ministers, attending continually upon this very thing."

Commentary: Paul extends the concept of submission to include the payment of taxes or tribute. He emphasizes that those who collect taxes are God's ministers, and their service supports the orderly functioning of society. Paying taxes is a civic responsibility that believers should fulfill conscientiously.

Verse 7

- "Render therefore to all their dues: tribute to whom tribute is due; custom to whom custom; fear to whom fear; honour to whom honour."

Commentary: Paul's instruction is clear: believers should fulfill their obligations to all authorities. This includes paying the required taxes and customs and showing appropriate respect and honor to those in positions of authority. This reflects a Christian's responsibility to be a law-abiding and respectful member of society.

Verse 8

- "Owe no man anything but to love one another: for he that loveth another hath fulfilled the law."

Commentary: Paul transitions from the topic of civil obligations to the principle of love. Believers are encouraged to live in a way that causes no harm or financial indebtedness to others. The only debt they should have is the debt of love. By loving one another, believers fulfill the law, emphasizing the centrality of love in Christian living.

Verse 9

- "For this, Thou shalt not commit adultery, Thou shalt not kill, Thou shalt not steal, Thou shalt not bear false witness, Thou shalt not covet; and if there be any other commandment, it is briefly comprehended in this saying, namely, Thou shalt love thy neighbour as thyself."

Commentary: Paul summarizes the moral requirements of the law by referencing several of the Ten Commandments. He underscores that love for one's neighbor encapsulates these commandments. By practicing love, believers naturally fulfill the moral law, reinforcing the idea that love is the fulfilling of the law.

Verse 10

- "Love worketh no ill to his neighbour: therefore love is the fulfilling of the law."

Commentary: Paul reiterates the central role of love in fulfilling the moral law. Love is described as non-injurious and non-harming towards one's neighbor. When believers love genuinely, they inherently fulfill the law's moral requirements by treating others with kindness, fairness, and respect.

Verse 11

- "And that, knowing the time, that now it is high time to awake out of sleep: for now is our salvation nearer than when we believed."

Commentary: Paul reminds believers of the urgency of the times. It is a call to spiritual awakening and vigilance. The phrase "our salvation nearer than when we believed" emphasizes the imminence of Christ's return and the final fulfillment of their salvation.

Verse 12

"The night is far spent, the day is at hand: let us, therefore, cast off the works of darkness, and let us put on the armour of light."

Commentary: Paul uses the metaphor of night and day to convey the idea that the present era is passing and the dawn of a new era is approaching with Christ's return. Believers are encouraged to cast off the behaviors associated with spiritual darkness and to clothe themselves with the armor of light, signifying the virtues of righteousness and truth.

Verse 13

- "Let us walk honestly, as in the day; not in rioting and drunkenness, not in chambering and wantonness, not in strife and envying."

Commentary: Paul exhorts believers to live honorably and transparently, as they would in the light of day. This involves abstaining from activities associated with darkness, such as excess in revelry, drunkenness, indulgence in sexual immorality (chambering and wantonness), and engagement in conflict and jealousy.

Romans 13:14: Putting on the Lord Jesus Christ

Verse 14

- "But put ye on the Lord Jesus Christ, and make not provision for the flesh, to fulfil the lusts thereof."

Commentary: In this single verse, Paul provides profound guidance on Christian living:

- "Put ye on the Lord Jesus Christ": This phrase encapsulates the essence of Christian transformation. To "put on" implies adopting or clothing oneself with the character and virtues of Christ. It means embracing His teachings, His example, and His righteousness. By putting on Christ, believers are called to align their lives with His life and imitate His love, humility, and obedience.

- "Make not provision for the flesh, to fulfil the lusts thereof": Paul warns against making allowances or provisions for the sinful nature, often referred to as the "flesh." Believers are called to be vigilant in not providing opportunities for sinful desires to take root and flourish. This involves avoiding situations or behaviors that could lead to sinful indulgence.

This verse emphasizes the transformative power of Christ's influence in a believer's life. It encourages an ongoing commitment to living in a manner consistent with His character and teachings. By doing so, believers resist the temptations of the flesh and seek to fulfill the will of God in their daily lives. The imagery of "putting on Christ" suggests a profound and ongoing relationship with Him and a conscious effort to reflect His image in thought, word, and deed.

CHAPTER 14
Principles for Dealing with Differences in the Church

Romans 14:1-10: Principles for Dealing with Differences in the Church

Verse 1

- "Him that is weak in the faith receive ye, but not to doubtful disputations."

Commentary: In this verse, Paul addresses the treatment of believers who may have weaker or more limited faith. He encourages the strong in faith to welcome and accept those who are less assured in their beliefs. He advises that they should not engage in contentious arguments or disputes over doubtful or disputable matters of faith.

Paul is emphasizing the importance of Christian unity and harmony even when there are differences in understanding.

Verse 2

- "For one believeth that he may eat all things: another, who is weak, eateth herbs."

Commentary: Paul gives an example of a disputable matter: the issue of dietary restrictions. Some believers feel free to eat any kind of food, while others, who are described as "weak," restrict their diet to vegetables or herbs. This difference in practice may stem from different convictions or understanding of Old Testament dietary laws.

Verse 3

- "Let not him that eateth despise him that eateth not; and let not him which eateth not judge him that eateth: for God hath received him."

Commentary: Paul cautions against judgment and disdain among believers on these matters. Those who have the liberty to eat should not look down on those who choose to follow dietary restrictions, and vice versa. The important point here is that God has received both, and their differing practices do not affect their standing in God's eyes.

Verse 4

- "Who art thou that judgest another man's servant? to his own master he standeth or falleth. Yea, he shall be holden up: for God is able to make him stand."

Commentary: Paul underscores the principle that individual believers are ultimately accountable to God, their Master, for their actions and convictions. Believers should avoid the role of judging or condemning one another, as it is God who upholds them. God has the power to support and make them stand in their faith.

Verse 5

- "One man esteemeth one day above another: another esteemeth every day alike. Let every man be fully persuaded in his own mind."

Commentary: Paul gives another example of a disputable matter, in this case, the observance of particular days. Some believers may regard certain days as more significant or holy than others, while others may treat all days the same. Paul's counsel is that each person should hold their convictions with full assurance in their own mind, but this should not lead to division or judgment within the community.

Verse 6

- "He that regardeth the day, regardeth it unto the Lord; and he that regardeth not the day, to the Lord he doth not regard it. He that eateth, eateth to the Lord, for he giveth God thanks; and he that eateth not, to the Lord he eateth not, and giveth God thanks."

Commentary: Here, Paul emphasizes that whether someone esteems a day or not, or eats certain foods or not, it should all be done to honor the Lord. In both cases, the believers offer thanks to God. This underscores that the heart of these actions should be devotion to God, not adherence to specific rules.

Verse 7

- "For none of us liveth to himself, and no man dieth to himself."

Commentary: Paul reminds believers that their lives are interconnected within the community of faith. Their actions and convictions have an impact not only on themselves but on others as well. This reinforces the idea that a believer's choices should consider the well-being and unity of the Christian community.

Verse 8

- "For whether we live, we live unto the Lord; and whether we die, we die unto the Lord: whether we live, therefore, or die, we are the Lord's."

Commentary: Paul emphasizes the overarching principle that both life and death belong to the Lord. Believers are wholly committed to God, and this devotion transcends matters of personal conviction or practice. It underscores that all believers are the possession of the Lord, and their lives should be lived for His glory.

Verse 9

- "For to this end Christ both died, and rose, and revived, that he might be Lord both of the dead and living."

Commentary: Paul relates these principles back to the work of Christ. He highlights that Christ's death and resurrection had a specific purpose: to establish His lordship over both the living and the dead. This reinforces the idea that the unity and well-being of the Christian community are essential to the lordship of Christ.

Verse 10

- "But why dost thou judge thy brother? or why dost thou set at nought thy brother? for we shall all stand before the judgment seat of Christ."

Commentary: Paul reiterates the question of why believers should judge or look down on their fellow believers. Ultimately, all believers will stand before the judgment seat of Christ, where each one's life and actions will be evaluated. This serves as a reminder that God is the ultimate judge, and it is not the role of one believer to condemn another for differences in personal convictions or practices.

These verses in Romans 14 provide important guidance on dealing with differences in matters of faith and personal convictions within the Christian community. Paul encourages unity, respect, and non-judgmental attitudes, emphasizing that each believer is ultimately accountable to God. The principles of love, devotion to the Lord, and recognition of Christ's lordship underscore the significance of maintaining harmony and mutual respect within the body of Christ.

Romans 14:11-22: Unity and Charity in Matters of Conscience

Verse 11

- "For it is written, As I live, saith the Lord, every knee shall bow to me, and every tongue shall confess to God."

Commentary: Paul begins this section by quoting from the Old Testament (Isaiah 45:23) to emphasize the ultimate recognition of God's sovereignty. Every person, believer or non-believer, will ultimately acknowledge God's authority and lordship. This underscores the importance of living in harmony and humility within the Christian community.

Verse 12

- "So then every one of us shall give account of himself to God."

Commentary: Paul reinforces the individual accountability of every believer to God. Regardless of differences in personal convictions or practices, each person will stand before God and give an account of their actions and choices. This should motivate believers to act with humility and avoid passing judgment on one another.

Verse 13

- "Let us not, therefore, judge one another anymore: but judge this rather, that no man put a stumbling block or an occasion to fall in his brother's way."

Commentary: Paul reiterates the principle of refraining from judgment among believers. Instead of passing judgment, the focus should be on avoiding actions or behavior that could cause another believer to stumble or be led into sin. This reflects the idea of prioritizing the spiritual well-being and unity of the Christian community.

Verse 14

- "I know, and am persuaded by the Lord Jesus, that there is nothing unclean of itself: but to him that esteemeth anything to be unclean, to him it is unclean."

Commentary: Paul addresses the issue of dietary practices and clarifies that, in and of themselves, there is nothing inherently unclean. However, he acknowledges that individual convictions and beliefs can influence one's perception. If someone believes something to be unclean, it becomes unclean in their conscience. This underscores the significance of respecting each other's convictions, even when they differ.

Verse 15

- "But if thy brother be grieved with thy meat, now walkest thou not charitably. Destroy not him with thy meat, for whom Christ died."

Commentary: Paul emphasizes the importance of love and charity in one's actions. If a fellow believer is distressed or grieved by another's dietary choices or practices, it is uncharitable to persist in those actions. In such cases, it is more important to avoid causing harm or stumbling to a brother or sister for whom Christ sacrificed Himself.

Verse 16

- "Let not then your good be evil spoken of:"

Commentary: Paul advises believers not to allow their freedom or liberty in matters of personal conviction to become a cause for criticism or slander by others. Instead, they should act in ways that demonstrate their love and respect for others, preserving their witness and reputation.

Verse 17

- "For the kingdom of God is not meat and drink, but righteousness, and peace, and joy in the Holy Ghost."

Commentary: Paul shifts the focus from external matters, such as dietary choices, to the core of the Christian faith. He underscores that the kingdom of God is not primarily concerned with what one eats or drinks but with righteousness (living in a right relationship with God and others), peace (harmony within the community of believers), and joy in the Holy Spirit (spiritual joy derived from one's relationship with God).

Verse 18

- "For he that in these things serveth Christ is acceptable to God, and approved of men."

Commentary: Paul emphasizes that those who prioritize righteousness, peace, and joy in the Holy Spirit are well-pleasing to God and earn the approval and respect of others. This is a testament to the transformative power of a Christ-centered life focused on these core values.

Verse 19

- "Let us, therefore, follow after the things which make for peace, and things wherewith one may edify another."

Commentary: Paul calls for a deliberate pursuit of actions that lead to peace and the building up of fellow believers. This highlights the importance of unity and the edification of one another in the Christian community.

Verse 20

- "For meat destroy not the work of God. All things indeed are pure, but it is evil for that man who eateth with offence."

Commentary: Paul reiterates that, in themselves, all foods are pure. However, if someone eats with offense, causing another to stumble or be offended, then it is not right. This underscores the importance of considering the impact of one's actions on the spiritual well-being of others.

Verse 21

- "It is good neither to eat flesh, nor to drink wine, nor anything whereby thy brother stumbleth, or is offended, or is made weak."

Commentary: Paul extends the principle to avoid anything that could cause a fellow believer to stumble, be offended, or become spiritually weak. This reinforces the concept of prioritizing love, unity, and the well-being of the Christian community over personal liberties.

Verse 22

- "Hast thou faith? Have it to thyself before God. Happy is he that condemneth not himself in that thing which he alloweth."

Commentary: Paul acknowledges that some may have a strong faith that permits certain practices or liberties. However, he advises believers to keep such convictions between themselves and God, without making a public display. The key is to maintain a clear conscience and avoid self-condemnation in the things they allow.

In these verses, Paul continues to address matters of conscience, emphasizing love, unity, and the avoidance of actions that could harm or offend fellow believers. He underscores the importance of prioritizing the well-being and spiritual growth of others over personal freedoms, recognizing that the ultimate goal is to live in harmony and love within the Christian community.

Romans 14:23: Faith and Conscience

Verse 23

- "And he that doubteth is damned if he eat, because he eateth not of faith: for whatsoever is not of faith is sin."

Commentary: This verse serves as a powerful conclusion to the discussion in Romans 14 about matters of conscience and Christian freedom:

- "And he that doubteth is damned if he eat": This statement suggests that if someone has doubts about whether a particular action, such as eating certain foods, is sinful, and they do it despite those doubts, they act without a clear conscience.

- "because he eateth not of faith": The phrase "not of faith" signifies that the action is not carried out with a strong, unwavering conviction that it is acceptable or pleasing to God. It reflects a lack of confidence in the action's moral rightness.

- "for whatsoever is not of faith is sin": Paul's overarching principle is that any action taken without a genuine, faith-based conviction that it aligns with God's will is considered a sin. This highlights the importance of faith and conscience in Christian living.

In this verse, Paul addresses the critical relationship between faith and conscience. He underscores that acting with a doubtful or troubled conscience, without a clear conviction of faith, can lead to moral guilt or sin. This reinforces the principle that believers should act in accordance with their genuine faith and convictions, all while respecting the faith and convictions of others in matters of conscience. It also highlights the importance of personal discernment and conscientious living within the Christian faith.

CHAPTER 15

The Example of Christ-Like Love and Unity

Romans 15:1-10: The Example of Christ-Like Love and Unity
Verse 1

- "We then that are strong ought to bear the infirmities of the weak, and not to please ourselves."

Commentary: In this verse, Paul addresses the responsibility of those who are spiritually mature and strong in their faith. He encourages them to support and help those who are weaker in their faith, rather than pursuing their own self-interests. This reflects the idea of selflessness and Christian charity.

Verse 2

- "Let every one of us please his neighbour for his good to edification."

Commentary: Paul emphasizes the importance of pleasing or serving one's neighbor for the purpose of their edification or spiritual growth. This underscores the idea of building up one another in faith and love.

Verse 3

- "For even Christ pleased not himself, but, as it is written, The reproaches of them that reproached thee fell on me."

Commentary: Paul points to the example of Christ, who did not seek His own pleasure but took on the reproaches and sufferings that were directed at God. This illustrates the self-sacrificing love of Christ, who bore the sins and reproaches of humanity on the cross.

Verse 4

- "For whatsoever things were written aforetime were written for our learning, that we through patience and comfort of the scriptures might have hope."

Commentary: Paul highlights the value of the Old Testament Scriptures, emphasizing that they were written for the instruction and learning of believers. He suggests that the patient study of the Scriptures can bring comfort and hope to those who seek God's guidance.

Verse 5

- "Now the God of patience and consolation grant you to be likeminded one toward another according to Christ Jesus:"

Commentary: Paul prays for believers to be of the same mind or to have unity, in line with the example set by Christ Jesus. He attributes this unity to the God of patience and consolation, emphasizing that God can grant believers the ability to harmonize in their faith and actions.

Verse 6

- "That ye may with one mind and one mouth glorify God, even the Father of our Lord Jesus Christ."

Commentary: Paul's prayer for unity among believers has a purpose—to collectively glorify God the Father, who is the Father of our Lord Jesus Christ. The idea of believers speaking with one mouth emphasizes their shared confession and praise of God.

Verse 7

- "Wherefore receive ye one another, as Christ also received us to the glory of God."

Commentary: Paul urges believers to welcome and accept one another, drawing on the example of how Christ received them. Just as Christ received believers into His family and grace, they should receive one another for the glory of God. This underscores the importance of hospitality, inclusion, and love within the Christian community.

Verse 8

- "Now I say that Jesus Christ was a minister of the circumcision for the truth of God, to confirm the promises made unto the fathers:"

Commentary: Paul emphasizes the role of Jesus Christ as a minister to the Jewish people, confirming the truth of God and fulfilling the promises made to the patriarchs and forefathers of the Jewish faith.

Verse 9

- "And that the Gentiles might glorify God for his mercy; as it is written, For this cause I will confess to thee among the Gentiles, and sing unto thy name."

Commentary: Paul highlights God's mercy to the Gentiles, allowing them to glorify God as well. He cites Old Testament passages that illustrate how the Gentiles would acknowledge and praise God's name.

Verse 10

- "And again he saith, Rejoice, ye Gentiles, with his people."

Commentary: Paul quotes another Old Testament passage that calls the Gentiles to rejoice alongside God's people. This demonstrates the inclusivity of the gospel, where both Jews and Gentiles can share in the joy of salvation through Christ.

In these verses, Paul emphasizes the principles of unity, selflessness, and Christ-like love within the Christian community. He draws on the example of Christ and the guidance of the Scriptures to encourage believers to serve and support one another. Additionally, he highlights the universality of the gospel, where both Jews and Gentiles can find hope and rejoicing in Christ. This section reinforces the importance of unity and mutual encouragement among believers.

Romans 15:11-20: Paul's Mission and the Gospel to the Gentiles

Verse 11

- "And again, Praise the Lord, all ye Gentiles; and laud him, all ye people."

Commentary: Paul continues to cite Old Testament passages that highlight the inclusion of the Gentiles in the worship and praise of God. This underscores the universality of the gospel message, which extends beyond the Jewish people.

Verse 12

- "And again, Esaias saith, There shall be a root of Jesse, and he that shall rise to reign over the Gentiles; in him shall the Gentiles trust."

Commentary: Paul references the prophet Isaiah's prediction regarding the Messiah, who would be a descendant of Jesse (King David's father) and would rule over the Gentiles. This prophecy anticipates the universal reign of Christ and the trust that the Gentiles would place in Him.

Verse 13

- "Now the God of hope fill you with all joy and peace in believing, that ye may abound in hope, through the power of the Holy Ghost."

Commentary: Paul offers a prayer for the Roman believers, invoking the "God of hope." He prays for them to experience joy and peace through their faith in Christ. The result of this is an abundance of hope, empowered by the Holy Spirit. This prayer emphasizes the role of faith, hope, and the Holy Spirit in the life of a believer.

Verse 14

- "And I myself also am persuaded of you, my brethren, that ye also are full of goodness, filled with all knowledge, able also to admonish one another."

Commentary: Paul expresses his confidence in the Roman believers, acknowledging their qualities of goodness, knowledge, and the ability to provide admonishment or counsel to one another. This reflects the mutual encouragement and edification that should exist within the Christian community.

Verse 15

- "Nevertheless, brethren, I have written the more boldly unto you in some sort, as putting you in mind, because of the grace that is given to me of God,"

Commentary: Paul acknowledges that he has written to the Romans boldly, perhaps emphasizing certain points or truths, because of the divine grace given to him by God. His intention is to remind and instruct them in light of his apostolic calling.

Verse 16

- "That I should be the minister of Jesus Christ to the Gentiles, ministering the gospel of God, that the offering up of the Gentiles might be acceptable, being sanctified by the Holy Ghost."

Commentary: Paul clarifies his ministry as an apostle to the Gentiles. He is dedicated to sharing the gospel of God with the Gentiles, with the aim of presenting them as an acceptable offering to God, sanctified by the Holy Spirit. This reflects Paul's mission to bring the Gentiles into a holy relationship with God.

Verse 17

- "I have, therefore, whereof I may glory through Jesus Christ in those things which pertain to God."

Commentary: Paul acknowledges that he can boast or glory in Jesus Christ regarding his ministry and his service to God. He recognizes that his work is inextricably tied to Christ and God's purposes.

Verse 18

- "For I will not dare to speak of any of those things which Christ hath not wrought by me, to make the Gentiles obedient, by word and deed,"

Commentary: Paul is careful not to speak of any achievements or actions that were not accomplished through Christ's working in him. His primary aim is to make the Gentiles obedient to the gospel through both his spoken words and his actions. This underscores the importance of leading by example in Christian ministry.

Verse 19

- "Through mighty signs and wonders, by the power of the Spirit of God; so that from Jerusalem, and round about unto Illyricum, I have fully preached the gospel of Christ."

Commentary: Paul references the signs and wonders performed through the power of the Spirit of God as evidence of the authenticity of his ministry. He has fully preached the gospel of Christ from Jerusalem to the region of Illyricum, encompassing a substantial geographical area.

Verse 20

- "Yea, so have I strived to preach the gospel, not where Christ was named, lest I should build upon another man's foundation:"

Commentary: Paul explains his evangelistic strategy, which was to preach the gospel in areas where Christ's name was not yet known. He wanted to avoid building on someone else's work or foundation, demonstrating his commitment to spreading the message to those who had not yet heard.

In these verses, Paul underscores the universality of the gospel message, emphasizing its reach to the Gentiles and the hope it brings. He also highlights his ministry, which includes both teaching and leading by example. Paul's mission is to make the Gentiles obedient to the gospel, and he has actively preached the gospel to regions where Christ was not yet named. His work serves as an inspiration for believers to share the message of Christ with those who have not yet heard.

Romans 15:21-30: Paul's Desire to Visit Rome and His Mission to the Saints

Verse 21

- "But as it is written, To whom he was not spoken of, they shall see: and they that have not heard shall understand."

Commentary: Paul cites the Old Testament prophecy from Isaiah 52:15, emphasizing that the message of the gospel, which was not previously known to some, will be made known, and those who had not heard will come to understand it. This reflects the universality of the gospel message and its impact on those who were previously unaware.

Verse 22

- "For which cause also I have been much hindered from coming to you."

Commentary: Paul explains that his commitment to spreading the gospel to regions where Christ was not known had hindered him from visiting the Roman Christians. His primary focus was on fulfilling his apostolic mission to reach those who had not yet heard about Christ.

Verse 23

- "But now, having no more place in these parts, and having a great desire these many years to come unto you;"

Commentary: Paul indicates that he has largely accomplished his mission in the regions he had been working in, and he has held a deep desire for many years to visit the Roman Christians. His yearning to visit Rome is motivated by his desire to strengthen and encourage the believers there.

Verse 24

- "Whensoever I take my journey into Spain, I will come to you: for I trust to see you in my journey, and to be brought on my way thitherward by you, if first I be somewhat filled with your company."

Commentary: Paul expresses his intention to visit Rome on his way to Spain, which was likely another region where he wished to spread the gospel. He anticipates that his visit to Rome will be a source of mutual encouragement, and he hopes to enjoy the fellowship of the Roman Christians before continuing his journey.

Verse 25

- "But now I go unto Jerusalem to minister unto the saints."

Commentary: Paul informs the Romans of his immediate plans to go to Jerusalem, where he intends to serve the needs of the Christian community, referred to as "the saints." This demonstrates his commitment to caring for fellow believers, particularly those in Jerusalem who may have been facing challenges.

Verse 26

- "For it hath pleased them of Macedonia and Achaia to make a certain contribution for the poor saints which are at Jerusalem."

Commentary: Paul mentions the generous contributions made by believers in Macedonia and Achaia for the benefit of the impoverished Christians in Jerusalem. This act of generosity and support reflects the unity and interconnectedness of the early Christian communities, as they extended help to those in need.

Verse 27

- "It hath pleased them verily, and their debtors they are. For if the Gentiles have been made partakers of their spiritual things, their duty is also to minister unto them in carnal things."

Commentary: Paul underscores the joy and responsibility of the believers from Macedonia and Achaia in providing assistance to their fellow believers in Jerusalem. He explains that since the Gentiles have shared in the spiritual blessings and teachings of the Jewish Christians, they should reciprocate by providing material support to those in Jerusalem.

Verse 28

- "When, therefore, I have performed this, and have sealed to them this fruit, I will come by you into Spain."

Commentary: Paul intends to complete this charitable mission to Jerusalem and present the financial assistance collected by the Gentile believers as a "fruit" of their faith. Afterward, he plans to visit the Romans on his way to Spain to continue his missionary work.

Verse 29

- "And I am sure that when I come unto you, I shall come in the fulness of the blessing of the gospel of Christ."

Commentary: Paul expresses his confidence that when he visits the Roman Christians, he will come with the fullness of God's blessings associated with the gospel of Christ. He envisions that his visit will bring spiritual blessings and further the work of the gospel in Rome.

Verse 30

- "Now I beseech you, brethren, for the Lord Jesus Christ's sake, and for the love of the Spirit, that ye strive together with me in your prayers to God for me;"

Commentary: Paul makes an earnest request to the Roman Christians, asking them to join him in prayer. He invokes the names of the Lord Jesus Christ and the love of the Spirit, emphasizing the importance of their prayers as he continues in his ministry and service to fellow believers.

In these verses, Paul reveals his missionary aspirations, his plans to visit the Roman Christians, and his ongoing commitment to ministering to the saints. He also highlights the spirit of generosity and support among different Christian communities and emphasizes the importance of prayer in the work of the gospel. Paul's desire is to strengthen the bonds among believers and continue the spread of the good news of Christ.

Romans 15:31-33: Paul's Prayer for Deliverance and Peace

Verse 31

- "That I may be delivered from them that do not believe in Judaea; and that my service which I have for Jerusalem may be accepted of the saints;"

Commentary: In this verse, Paul seeks prayer support from the Romans. He requests deliverance from those in Judea who do not believe, implying potential opposition or danger. He also desires that his service and the financial assistance he's bringing to Jerusalem will be accepted with joy and gratitude by the Christian community in Jerusalem.

Verse 32

- "That I may come unto you with joy by the will of God, and may with you be refreshed."

Commentary: Paul's second request is for a joyful and safe journey to Rome, as he intends to come to the Romans through God's will. He longs for a mutually refreshing and encouraging visit with the believers in Rome. This reflects his desire for fellowship and unity among Christians.

Verse 33

- "Now the God of peace be with you all. Amen."

Commentary: Paul closes this chapter with a prayer for the Romans, invoking God as the "God of peace." He asks for God's presence and peace to be with all the Roman believers. The word "Amen" is an affirmation of the prayer's validity.

In these final verses of Romans 15, Paul seeks support in prayer, both for his safety and acceptance in Jerusalem and for his joyful and refreshing visit to the Romans. His ultimate desire is for the God of peace to be with the entire Roman community. This chapter showcases Paul's heart for unity and love among believers and emphasizes the role of prayer and God's peace in Christian fellowship and ministry.

CHAPTER 16
Greetings and Commendations

Romans 16:1-10: Greetings and Commendations

Verse 1

- "I commend unto you Phebe our sister, which is a servant of the church which is at Cenchrea:"

Commentary: Paul begins this chapter by introducing Phebe, a sister in the faith and a servant of the church in Cenchrea, a port city near Corinth. By commending her to the Roman Christians, he highlights her significance in the Christian community and prepares the Romans to welcome her.

Verse 2

- "That ye receive her in the Lord, as becometh saints, and that ye assist her in whatsoever business she hath need of you: for she hath been a succourer of many, and of myself also."

Commentary: Paul instructs the Roman believers to receive Phebe with the respect and honor that is fitting for saints. He asks them to provide assistance to her in any matter she requires. Paul acknowledges Phebe's track record of assisting and supporting many individuals, including himself. This speaks to her reputation for acts of kindness and service within the Christian community.

Verse 3

- "Greet Priscilla and Aquila my helpers in Christ Jesus:"

Commentary: Paul extends greetings to Priscilla and Aquila, a husband and wife team who played a significant role in the early Christian church. They are noted as his "helpers in Christ Jesus," indicating their partnership in ministry alongside Paul.

Verse 4

- "Who have for my life laid down their own necks: unto whom not only I give thanks, but also all the churches of the Gentiles."

Commentary: Paul underscores the remarkable sacrifice Priscilla and Aquila made for his life, risking their own safety. He expresses gratitude to them and mentions that not only he but all the Gentile churches are thankful for their service and commitment.

Verse 5

- "Likewise greet the church that is in their house. Salute my well-beloved Epaenetus, who is the firstfruits of Achaia unto Christ."

Commentary: Paul sends greetings to the church that meets in the house of Priscilla and Aquila, emphasizing the importance of small house churches in the early Christian community. He also salutes Epaenetus, who is noted as the "firstfruits of Achaia unto Christ," likely indicating that Epaenetus was among the first converts in that region.

Verse 6

- "Greet Mary, who bestowed much labour on us."

Commentary: Paul greets Mary, acknowledging her significant efforts and labor on behalf of the Christian community. Her service may have included various forms of ministry and support.

Verse 7

- "Salute Andronicus and Junia, my kinsmen, and my fellow-prisoners, who are of note among the apostles, who also were in Christ before me."

Commentary: Paul sends greetings to Andronicus and Junia, who are not only fellow believers but also his relatives. They were imprisoned with Paul and are recognized as notable among the apostles. The mention that they were in Christ before Paul suggests their early conversion to Christianity.

Verse 8

- "Greet Amplias my beloved in the Lord."

Commentary: Paul extends greetings to Amplias, whom he affectionately refers to as "my beloved in the Lord." This reflects the strong bonds of love and fellowship within the early Christian community.

Verse 9

- "Salute Urbane, our helper in Christ, and Stachys my beloved."

Commentary: Paul greets Urbane, acknowledging him as a helper in Christ, likely indicating his active service in the Christian community. He also sends greetings to Stachys, whom he terms "my beloved," signifying their close relationship.

Verse 10

- "Salute Apelles approved in Christ. Salute them which are of Aristobulus' household."

Commentary: Paul greets Apelles, describing him as "approved in Christ," suggesting his proven faith and character. He also extends greetings to the members of Aristobulus' household, emphasizing the interconnectedness of the Christian community within households.

In these verses, Paul concludes the book of Romans by offering greetings and commendations to various individuals who played important roles in the early Christian community. He highlights their service, sacrifices, and contributions to the spread of the gospel. This section underscores the sense of community and fellowship within the early church and serves as a reminder of the diverse and devoted individuals who helped establish and strengthen the faith in various regions.

Romans 16:11-20: Greetings and Warnings

Verse 11

- "Salute Herodion my kinsman. Greet them that be of the household of Narcissus, which are in the Lord."

Commentary: Paul sends greetings to Herodion, who is noted as his kinsman, indicating a family connection. He also greets those in the household of Narcissus who are part of the Lord's community, acknowledging the presence of believers within this particular household.

Verse 12

- "Salute Tryphena and Tryphosa, who labour in the Lord. Salute the beloved Persis, which laboured much in the Lord."

Commentary: Paul salutes Tryphena and Tryphosa, both of whom are described as those who labor in the Lord. This suggests their active involvement in the work of the church. He also greets Persis, whom he calls "the beloved" and acknowledges for her extensive labor in the service of the Lord.

Verse 13

- "Salute Rufus chosen in the Lord, and his mother and mine."

Commentary: Paul extends greetings to Rufus, referring to him as "chosen in the Lord." This may suggest Rufus's prominence and dedication in the Christian community. He also mentions Rufus's mother as someone who is like a mother to him, highlighting their close relationship within the faith.

Verse 14

- "Salute Asyncritus, Phlegon, Hermas, Patrobas, Hermes, and the brethren which are with them."

Commentary: Paul offers greetings to several individuals and groups: Asyncritus, Phlegon, Hermas, Patrobas, Hermes, and the brethren who are associated with them. This demonstrates the interconnectedness and the sense of community among believers.

Verse 15

- "Salute Philologus, and Julia, Nereus, and his sister, and Olympas, and all the saints which are with them."

Commentary: Paul extends greetings to more individuals: Philologus, Julia, Nereus, and his sister, and Olympas, along with all the saints in their company. This emphasizes the collective identity of believers and their unity in Christ.

Verse 16

- "Salute one another with an holy kiss. The churches of Christ salute you."

Commentary: Paul encourages believers to greet one another with a holy kiss, a common practice in the early church symbolizing love and fellowship. He also mentions that the churches of Christ send their greetings to the Roman Christians, illustrating the interconnectedness of Christian communities.

Verse 17

- "Now I beseech you, brethren, mark them which cause divisions and offences contrary to the doctrine which ye have learned, and avoid them."

Commentary: Paul transitions from greetings to a serious exhortation. He urges the Roman believers to pay attention to and identify those who cause divisions and offenses that go against the teachings they have received. He instructs them to avoid such individuals, emphasizing the importance of doctrinal unity and harmony within the church.

Verse 18

- "For they that are such serve not our Lord Jesus Christ, but their own belly, and by good words and fair speeches deceive the hearts of the simple."

Commentary: Paul explains that those who cause divisions and offenses are not serving the Lord Jesus Christ but are driven by self-interest and personal gain. They use persuasive language to deceive the naïve or simple-hearted. This serves as a warning against false teachers and those who seek to disrupt the unity of the church.

Verse 19

- "For your obedience is come abroad unto all men. I am glad, therefore, on your behalf: but yet I would have you wise unto that which is good and simple concerning evil."

Commentary: Paul commends the Roman believers for their obedience, which is known to others. He is pleased with their faithfulness. However, he advises them to be wise in what is good and innocent in recognizing evil. This means they should discern between right and wrong, while maintaining a pure and simple faith.

Verse 20

- "And the God of peace shall bruise Satan under your feet shortly. The grace of our Lord Jesus Christ be with you. Amen."

Commentary: Paul provides words of encouragement, promising that the God of peace will soon crush Satan under their feet. This is a reference to the ultimate victory of Christ over the forces of evil. He concludes with a prayer for the grace of the Lord Jesus Christ to be with the Roman believers, affirming the truth of his message with the word "Amen."

In these verses, Paul balances greetings with a serious warning about divisive individuals within the church. He encourages the believers to remain faithful, discerning, and united. Paul's words serve as a reminder of the importance of maintaining doctrinal purity and unity while continuing in love and fellowship within the Christian community.

Romans 16:21-27: Final Greetings and Doxology

Verse 21

- "Timotheus my workfellow, and Lucius, and Jason, and Sosipater, my kinsmen, salute you."

Commentary: Paul sends greetings from several individuals, including Timothy (Timotheus), whom he refers to as a workfellow. He also mentions Lucius, Jason, and Sosipater, indicating their connection to him as kinsmen. These greetings further underscore the sense of community and the bonds between early Christians.

Verse 22

- "I Tertius, who wrote this epistle, salute you in the Lord."

Commentary: Tertius, who acted as the scribe writing down Paul's words, sends his greetings to the Romans. His inclusion in the greeting reflects the collaborative nature of Paul's ministry and the importance of those who worked alongside him.

Verse 23

- "Gaius, mine host, and of the whole church, saluteth you. Erastus, the chamberlain of the city, saluteth you, and Quartus, a brother."

Commentary: Paul mentions Gaius, who is not only his host but is also recognized as hosting the entire church. Erastus, the chamberlain (city treasurer) of the city, extends greetings, indicating that even those in official positions acknowledge the Christian community. Quartus is described as a brother, emphasizing the familial bonds within the faith.

Verse 24

- "The grace of our Lord Jesus Christ be with you all. Amen."

Commentary: Paul concludes this section with a prayer for the grace of the Lord Jesus Christ to be with all the Roman believers, reaffirming the importance of God's grace in the life of a Christian.

Verse 25

- "Now to him that is of power to stablish you according to my gospel, and the preaching of Jesus Christ, according to the revelation of the mystery, which was kept secret since the world began,"

Commentary: This verse introduces a doxology, a hymn of praise. Paul acknowledges God's power to establish or strengthen the Roman believers according to the gospel he preached. This gospel centers on Jesus Christ and reveals a mystery that was kept hidden since the world's beginning.

Verse 26

- "But now is made manifest, and by the scriptures of the prophets, according to the commandment of the everlasting God, made known to all nations for the obedience of faith:"

Commentary: Paul emphasizes that this mystery is now revealed and made known through the scriptures of the prophets. It aligns with the commandment of the eternal God and is proclaimed to all nations, with the goal of bringing about obedience rooted in faith.

Verse 27

- "To God only wise, be glory through Jesus Christ forever. Amen."

Commentary: Paul concludes with a declaration of praise. He attributes wisdom and glory to God alone, and this glory is given through Jesus Christ eternally. The word "Amen" confirms the truth and certainty of this declaration.

In these verses, Paul's final greetings highlight the interconnectedness and unity of the early Christian community. He also offers a doxology, praising God for revealing the mystery of the gospel through the scriptures of the prophets. This doxology underscores the importance of faith and obedience, and it concludes with a declaration of glory to God through Jesus Christ. It serves as a fitting conclusion to the Book of Romans, celebrating the profound truths and doctrines presented throughout the letter.

CONCLUSION

The Book of Romans is a profound and spiritually enriching letter, authored by the Apostle Paul, and it holds a unique and cherished place within the New Testament. It is a comprehensive exposition of Christian theology, doctrine, and practice that has shaped the understanding of the faith for centuries. This remarkable epistle is a theological masterpiece that continues to impact believers' lives, shape Christian thought, and provide a profound understanding of God's redemptive plan.

The Book of Romans commences with a powerful declaration that all of humanity is in need of redemption due to sin. Paul emphasizes the universality of sin, both among Jews and Gentiles, leveling the ground before God. This foundational truth underscores the significance of grace, as no one can earn their salvation by human effort.

Paul proceeds to explore the concept of justification by faith in Romans 3-4. This theme is a cornerstone of Christian doctrine, highlighting that righteousness is imputed through faith in Christ. This truth liberates believers from the burden of self-justification, offering assurance of salvation and reconciliation with God.

Chapter 5 continues to illuminate the depth of God's love, demonstrated through Christ's sacrifice. The stark contrast between Adam's sin and Christ's righteousness is drawn, revealing that where sin leads to death, God's grace leads to eternal life.

Romans 6 delves into the believer's identification with Christ's death and resurrection, highlighting the transformative power of grace in sanctification. The call to present oneself as an instrument of righteousness serves as a reminder of the ongoing process of becoming more like Christ.

Paul's honest portrayal of the inner struggles of a believer in Romans 7 emphasizes the ongoing battle with sin. It underscores the necessity of the Holy Spirit in the believer's life, revealing that through Christ, we are set free from the power of sin.

The rich insights of Romans 8 offer a profound sense of assurance and hope to believers. The Holy Spirit's role in intercession, God's unwavering love, and the security of those called according to His purpose provide a deep sense of confidence and peace.

The latter chapters of Romans provide practical instructions for Christian living. Paul emphasizes the importance of love, humility, and submission to authorities. These chapters guide believers in applying the principles of faith and grace to their everyday lives.

In the grand finale of Romans, Paul expresses his love for the Roman believers and his earnest desire for unity within the church. These closing remarks demonstrate the significance of Christian fellowship and emphasize the communal aspect of the faith.

The Book of Romans remains a timeless treasure of Christian literature. Its theological depth, spiritual insights, and practical guidance continue to inspire and instruct believers. It has profoundly influenced the development of Christian doctrine, from the early Church Fathers to the Protestant Reformation and beyond.

Romans is a theological and devotional masterpiece that highlights the essential elements of the Christian faith: the universality of sin, justification by faith, God's redeeming love, the transformative power of grace, and the indwelling of the Holy Spirit. It offers believers the assurance of salvation, the hope of transformation, and the promise of an unbreakable relationship with God.

The latter chapters of Romans contain practical instructions for Christian living, emphasizing the importance of love, humility, and submission to authorities. Paul's closing remarks convey his love for the Roman believers and his desire for unity within the church.

In conclusion, the Book of Romans stands as a theological masterpiece that beautifully articulates the essence of the Christian faith. It highlights the pivotal role of faith, grace, and God's love in the believer's journey. Romans encourages us to live a life of faith, hope, and love, reflecting the transformative power of the gospel. Its enduring impact on Christian theology and its relevance in today's world continue to make it a cherished and essential part of the New Testament, offering a timeless message of salvation, transformation, and the unshakable love of God.

www.ingramcontent.com/pod-product-compliance
Lightning Source LLC
Chambersburg PA
CBHW071247150726
48001CB00018B/397